Desktops as a Service

Everything You Need to Know About DaaS & Hosted VDI

2014 Edition

Brian Madden
Gabe Knuth

Desktops as a Service

Everything You Need to Know About DaaS & Hosted VDI

2014 Edition

Published by
Burning Troll Productions, LLC
San Francisco, California
www.bmad.com/daasbook

Written by
Brian Madden
Gabe Knuth

Reviewer
Jack Madden

Project Manager
Marya Lyons

Copy Editor
Monica Sambataro

Paperback ISBN 978-0-9852174-2-6

Set in Chaparral Light, 11 over 13

First Edition, March 2014

Contents

From the Authors

Gabe Knuth:

I'm starting to feel like an old, salty veteran in this space that I've been covering since the very beginning of my career, but it changes so much it's hard to get too cynical. The day I graduated from a desktop support person to a highfalutin server guy was the day I met Brian. That morning, he said, "I'm going to a hospital to do a POC for this thing called MetaFrame. Wanna tag along?" The only word I knew in that sentence was "hospital," but I tagged along anyway and the rest is history. The day that I got out of desktops, I got pulled right back in, and that means I've spent every day of my 17-year career focused on delivering desktops and applications to users.

This book couldn't have been written without Brian or without the many interviews that we had with people from all around the industry, but most of all it required the support of my family. Many thanks go to my wife, Kaylene, son, Carson, and daughter, Elizabeth, for putting up with me furiously typing away in my office while they took care of everyday life. I used to do this stuff just for me, but now I do it for you guys, too. Love you all!

Brian Madden:

Let me tell you about how I remember the day I met Gabe. It was 1998, and I remember our first meeting as the night before we went to that hospital to do our first-ever MetaFrame installation. Gabe and I worked together at Vanstar in Cleveland. We were both under 21, and he knew a bar that wouldn't check IDs. "Follow me," he said. The next 20 minutes were a high-speed car chase as I tried not to lose him, me in my Saab 900 Turbo and Gabe in what I remember to be a royal blue Chevy Z-something he seemed to be very proud of.

"What's this kid trying to prove?" I thought as we weaved in and out of traffic on I-480. I rolled my eyes as I thought about all the cars that would be more appropriate for him. Saab 900, Saab 9000, heck, even a 3-series.

Once we got to the bar, we became fast friends, and the rest is history. Thanks to him for being my best buddy for the past 16 years!

And thanks to my other friends who have the sense enough to live in San Francisco. Paul, Andrew, Jack, Samantha, Maren, and Elena, see, I really was working on a book! It wasn't just an excuse to blow you all off over the past few months!

Gabe Knuth (Reprise):

It was a 1992 Chevy Cavalier Z24, in Medium Maui Metallic, and it only seemed like I was driving fast because Brian drives like an old man.

Acknowledgements

We'd like to thank all the wonderful folks who agreed to speak with us as we researched this book. Since DaaS is so new, we had a lot to learn as we wrote this, and we're grateful to those folks who work as DaaS providers, customers, and industry consultants who made sure we understood this industry.

To be clear, we're not suggesting the following people agree with everything we wrote, or even that we accurately captured their thoughts. But everyone here* gave us their time, and for that, thanks!

Danny Allan
Shawn Bass
Guise Bule
Paul Calvert
Jon Cellini
Mike Chase
Rick Dehlinger
Paul Duffy
Denis Gundarev
Ian Hutchinson
Harry Labana
Jack Madden
Ken Oestreich
Ron Oglesby
David Stafford
Benny Tritsch

*Plus a few others who asked that we not share their names.

1. Introduction to DaaS

If you're holding this book in your hands we assume you're interested in this thing called Desktops as a Service. Actually, maybe that's not a fair assumption. Maybe you or someone around you has heard of DaaS because your boss has recently barged into your office shouting, "Johnson! We're moving to DaaS! You're in charge!!"

Regardless of whether you came to learn about DaaS via your own free will or the simple desire to keep your job, the important thing is that you care about it. No matter if you want DaaS to succeed or fail, or you're here to just laugh at those trying it—you care!

The reality is that DaaS is a hot topic right now. If you thought VDI (virtual desktop infrastructure, in case you weren't aware) was hot because it involves end-user computing, mobility, and virtualization, DaaS takes all that *and* adds in the cloud! The success of DaaS is guaranteed! (Well, that's if you define "success" as having lots of bloggers write about it and people argue about it on Twitter.)

What Is DaaS?

Before we get too far into the book we should probably define our topic. We define DaaS simply as remote Windows desktops you pay someone else to host. Sometimes your users only see single applications, and sometimes they see complete desktops. Either way, there's a Windows desktop running on some provider's hardware that you're paying for as a service.

Some providers call this DaaS, while others call it hosted virtual desktops (or HVD), cloud desktops, hosted Windows desktops, or any one of dozens of other marketing-type words. For the purposes of this book, we're going to use the term "DaaS" to describe remote Windows desktops that you pay someone else to host, but keep in mind your provider might call it something else.

In most cases, DaaS providers use VDI technology to connect users to desktops that run a Windows client OS (like Windows 7 or Windows 8) and run as virtual machines in the provider's data center. Sometimes DaaS desktops are based on Windows Server OSes, and sometimes the DaaS providers hide the desktops and just deliver Windows applications on their own, but the gist is always the same. You give the DaaS provider some money. The provider gives you a URL or some client software. Your users push a button, log in, and see their own full Windows desktop, complete with their applications, their settings, and their files.

Since the vast majority of DaaS is based on VDI technology, understanding DaaS means understanding VDI. (We could have just as easily defined DaaS as VDI that you pay someone else to host.)

The problem with VDI is that it's expensive, since you have to buy a bunch of servers and storage to run your users' desktop VMs, and it's really complicated to get built and tuned properly. This is where DaaS providers come in. DaaS is just the providers saying, "Hey, you want to use VDI, but it's complex and expensive. How about if we build and host VDI for you and you just pay us this amount of money each month for each user? Sound good?"

That's VDI as a Service. That's DaaS.

The key is that DaaS is *not* a technology but rather simply a business decision around how you acquire and pay for VDI. After all, if you think VDI makes sense, why not buy it from the experts who really know what they're doing?

What DaaS Isn't

While we're on the topic of talking about what DaaS is, we should also talk about what it isn't. For the purposes of this book, DaaS is all about Microsoft Windows desktops and applications.

Though sometimes referred to as a cloud desktop, DaaS is not the same thing as the "web desktops" or "browser desktops" you read about on Slashdot. Those try to replicate the structure of a Windows desktop via HTML. You log in to the web desktop and you have a Start button, menus for applications, a wallpaper image, and links to other web apps, among other things.

These features are cute, and they might be great for our parents, who may know how to do things only one way, but these are not "desktops" in the enterprise sense. Really they're nothing more than fancy web-based bookmark tools with some scripts to make Dropbox look like Windows Explorer. Again, not that we're disparaging them. Web desktops can be cool for certain users. But when we talk about DaaS, we're talking about Microsoft Windows desktop environments running Windows desktop applications that you pay someone else to host.

While we're at it we should also address the Microsoft Windows aspect of our definition of DaaS. While it's true that several DaaS providers have options to deliver Linux-based VDI desktops and applications, the vast majority of today's enterprise desktops are Microsoft Windows-based desktops, and the desktop applications we have to support in the enterprise are Microsoft Windows-based desktop applications.

This is not to knock Linux—we would love nothing more than to not have a monopoly in the desktop space—but the reality of the enterprise world today is that desktop applications are Windows applications.

That said, probably 95% of the DaaS issues we address in this book are perfectly applicable to Linux-based desktops too. So if your world is full of Linux desktops and applications running the traditional way, you also have the option of building VDI to deliver that Linux environment from your data center or the option of paying a DaaS provider to deliver your Linux environment from their data center.

Why Now?

There's a lot of momentum in the industry, which makes 2014 a good time to talk about DaaS. Not least is that companies (even huge enterprises) are getting to be much more comfortable with outsourcing key IT systems to ~~service providers~~ (err, "cloud providers"). Ten years ago we all ran our own Exchange servers, file servers, CRM systems, and such. But now? We pay Google to host our email, we use Salesforce from the cloud, and we use Box for files. So really moving our desktops to the cloud and paying someone else to run them is just a logical extension to what we've been doing anyway. (And, by extension, if you say "No way, no way, no way!" to moving your email, collaboration, and file-sharing services to the cloud, you can put this book down now because there's no way you're going to move your desktops to the cloud!)

DaaS Won't Solve All Your Desktop Problems

From a high level, DaaS sounds great! You get all the benefits of VDI without the cost and hassle of buying, building, or running it yourself. Huzzah!

But there are some downsides and major caveats to DaaS too. First of all, remember that DaaS is just VDI that you pay for, right? You probably know that VDI hasn't exactly had a stunning success record since the concept was first introduced eight years ago. Worldwide adoption rates of VDI are somewhere in the 1% to 3% range (depending on whose data you trust), and we haven't exactly seen any companies beating down the door to convert 100% of their users from traditional desktops and laptops to VDI.

"But guys," you might argue, "that's because VDI is *hard*. If you're using DaaS, the provider does all the hard work!" It's a fair point. After all, what do you have to know about running an email system to outsource your email to Google? That's the whole point, right?

And to be fair, the DaaS providers *do* handle all of the hard back-end work of VDI. If you want to use DaaS, you can visit a website, type in your credit card number, and be using a full Microsoft Windows desktop—delivered through your web browser—inside of a few minutes. You don't have to know anything about the DaaS provider's hardware, brokering software, storage, network, protocol, security, or backup plan.

So that's awesome! But take a step back. What exactly are you getting from your DaaS provider? It is literally *just* a desktop. Where are your applications? Where are your files? How do you print? How do you get your drives mapped? How do you hook up your email? If you change your password at work, how does the DaaS password change?

This brings us to our second major point: DaaS is *just* a desktop. Remember that DaaS stands for Desktops as a Service, not "Full Desktop Engineering as a Service" or "Fully Configured and Supported Desktop Exactly As You Want It as a Service."

Many DaaS providers advertise their services by saying something like, "We give you a VDI desktop that's as easy to use as just knowing where the power switch is on your traditional desktop PC!" That ad copy is not a joke! That is literally what they offer. (Actually, in most cases it's *all* they offer.) The DaaS provider is responsible for connecting your users to their desktops. What happens once they're connected is up to you. (Well, it is possible to buy additional services from some DaaS providers. We'll get into that more later.)

To understand the significance of this, think about the last desktop migration or desktop rollout you did. We can imagine that the initial stages of provisioning a desktop for a user involved installing Windows, adding it to the domain, running Windows update, etc. (Or maybe these initial stages were done by imaging the new desktop PC from your master image.) Once it's ready to go, you physically took the computer to the user's desk and turned it on.

But at the point of when you power on the new desktop for the user, how far along are you in terms of that user's migration? Maybe 10% or 20%. Because even after you get the initial computer built, you still have to install all of the user's departmental and custom apps. You have to get the user's files copied over and the user profile set up. You need to figure out how you're going to patch, update, and maintain this thing.

And this doesn't even include all of the back-end engineering that took place before you dropped the new computer on the user's desk. If you transitioned from Windows XP to Windows 7, you had months (or years) of behind-the-scenes work figuring out your profile migration, application testing and updating, security changes, and drivers, among other things.

DaaS is no different. Yeah, your DaaS provider can give you nearly instant access to hundreds of brand new Windows 7 desktops. But if your existing environment is Windows XP with ten years of user customizations (which are different for each user), the moment you first connect to your sparkling new DaaS environment represents a point that's probably only 20% of the way to your end goal of desktop migration.

This, by the way, is not a lesson that we're just learning with DaaS. This is something we learned five years ago with VDI. Back when companies first started experimenting with VDI, many of them failed, not because they couldn't handle the raw infrastructure, but because they had all these grandiose plans about how they were going to change the way they managed desktops once they got to VDI and it turned out that those management changes were more than they could handle.

For example, many early proponents of VDI claimed VDI was more manageable than traditional PCs because with VDI, multiple users could share a single desktop image via something called desktop pooling, or non-persistent images. The problem is that traditional Windows desktop and laptop environments don't work this way, since each user has his or her own desktop with its own applications. So if you want to convert from persistent traditional desktop PCs to non-persistent VDI desktops, that's a big freaking deal! Making non-persistent VDI images work means you have to factor in all sorts of new things, like application virtualization and user profile management and image pool management and layering, none of which work 100% in every environment. This ultimately leads to failed VDI implementations because the environments aren't as flexible as what people had before VDI.

In other words, the vast majority of VDI environments failed to meet expectations not because of the "VDI-ness" of them, but because the people doing the projects bit off more than they could chew. And guess what? DaaS projects risk the same fate! It's just so tempting to want to change, change, change, and before you know it you have a humongous project with no chance of success.

Does this mean that we think DaaS is bad? Certainly not! We love DaaS! It's just important to remember that all DaaS does is deliver the VDI or Windows desktop infrastructure. How you migrate, operate, and maintain those Windows desktops is still up to you.

As a side note, we understand that some people reading this book might be thinking, "But I don't want to worry about Windows. I want to outsource my entire desktop environment, including all the management of it." That's awesome! (And congrats to you for being able to do that!) If you're looking for desktop outsourcing, that's great, but that's not DaaS. That's IT outsourcing or using a managed service provider or something. (Now, if you do take that route, you may find that your outsourcer chooses to use VDI or DaaS as the way to deliver the desktops they're managing to your users. Again, that's perfectly fine.) The key is that when you're shopping around for DaaS providers and one quotes you $35 per user per month, you need to recognize that that's not full desktop outsourcing—that's just the delivery of the raw desktop container.

The other important thing to know about DaaS up front is that we don't believe your decision around whether to use it has to be an all-or-nothing approach. For example, we've written quite a bit about how we believe that VDI is just an alternate form factor of a Windows desktop. In most cases we don't believe it makes sense for a company to move to VDI for 100% of its users, and many of today's most successful VDI projects involve only a subset of a company's users.

So, since DaaS is just VDI we're paying someone else for, we like to take the same approach with it. When considering DaaS, we first want you to figure out where VDI makes sense in your organization and where it doesn't. Once you figure out which of your users are good candidates for VDI, then you can figure out whether it makes sense to build and operate the VDI yourself (traditional VDI) or whether you want to pay someone else to build and operate it for you (DaaS).

In other words, we're big fans of thinking about (and getting excited about) VDI first. Once you're on board with VDI, you can consider DaaS.

Of course once you're there, we believe DaaS has a lot to get excited about! In fact, we believe that in the majority of cases, it probably *does* make sense for you to pay a DaaS provider to host your VDI. After all, they're the experts at VDI. They have the scale to get good deals on hardware, power, and cooling. They have great relationships with Citrix, VMware, and Microsoft. They have architects and engineers who focus exclusively on VDI. They can build and operate VDI that's cheaper, more secure, and more reliable than you can.

Paying for VDI from a DaaS provider has the same soft benefits as paying for other cloud services, like low up-front costs, granular scalability, and the ability to be up and running in days instead of months. For example, if you build your own VDI, you might have to buy tens or hundreds of thousands of dollars' worth of hardware just to get started. With DaaS, you simply pay the monthly costs for the exact number of users you need to set up. If you need to add ten users in the future, you know exactly how much it's going to cost and you can get them up and running instantly. Compare that with running your own VDI environment, where you might have to buy additional hardware, wait for it to arrive, and then build and configure it. With DaaS, if you later want to stop using VDI for some users, you simply cancel their accounts and stop paying. With VDI, you own that hardware whether you use it or not.

DaaS Challenges

So DaaS is awesome, right? Yes! But like with everything, there are some drawbacks.

First is that like with any outsourcing or cloud-based offering, you have to be comfortable putting your data and desktops in the cloud. You have to be comfortable trusting someone else, which includes their employees, their hardware, and their buildings. You have to trust their unknowns. You have to trust that they're not going to go out of business overnight and that they have good policies in place to protect the security of your data. You have to trust that they've taken measures to ensure that the VDI desktops they're hosting for you are going to be available when you need them.

Once you find a DaaS provider you trust, you have to work out the logistics of how your desktops—running in the DaaS provider's cloud—are going to connect back into your existing on-premises computing environment. When you build your own VDI, your VDI desktops are in your own data center, right next to your file and application servers. But if you move your VDI into someone else's data center, how do those desktop users access their data? Do you move all of your files into the cloud as well? Do you keep your files in your own data center and then open up some kind of VPN tunnel between it and the DaaS provider? What about your domain controllers? How will these decisions affect performance?

These are the questions and logistical issues that we're going to address in this book. The bottom line is that we love DaaS, and we think it makes a lot of sense for a lot of users. But we also understand DaaS's place in the world and that it's not for everyone.

At the end of the day, we want everyone to make the desktop hosting decisions that work for them. If we can keep people from going to DaaS when it's not right, that's good for us because we have the benefit of more happy users in the world. And if we can help people see that they should be outsourcing the operation of their VDI environments to DaaS providers, then we're excited that we can help them focus on more interesting things.

So let's take a look at what you need to do to be successful with DaaS!

2. The Promise (and Reality) of VDI

In the previous chapter we talked about how we think about DaaS and how to frame it in your mind in ways that maximize your chances of success. We explained that we believe that DaaS is nothing more than Windows desktops that you pay someone else to host, and that in most cases those desktops are hosted with VDI technology.

So that means our conversation about DaaS needs to start with a discussion about VDI, which is going to be the focus of the next few chapters. We need to look at the technology behind VDI, where VDI works and where it doesn't, and how to be successful with it. Then (and only then) can we have the real DaaS conversation, which goes something like this: "Okay, so you decided that VDI makes sense for some of your users. Great! Now how do you decide whether you want to build that yourself (which is traditional on-premises VDI) or pay someone else to host it for you (which is VDI as a Service, also known as DaaS)."

We (Brian Madden and Gabe Knuth, the authors of this book) actually wrote a book about VDI (along with a third author, Jack Madden) in 2012, called "The VDI Delusion." We also wrote an update to the first edition last year, called "The New VDI Reality." If you haven't read either of these books, we recommend that you do, since again, DaaS is VDI, and to be successful at DaaS, you have to be successful at VDI! You can buy the books on Amazon, or if you Google search for them, you can probably find illegal copies posted somewhere. At this point we don't really care how you get our VDI books. We just care that you read them. (Check out bmad.com/vdibook to obtain a legal copy.)

For those of you who don't want to read these books, or it's been awhile since you have, we're going to start with an overview of what you need to know about VDI. If you really, really think you already know VDI, you can skip right to the chapters on DaaS on the condition that you can pass the following quiz.

Answer true or false for the following statements:

1. VDI is easier to manage than traditional desktops.
2. VDI is more secure than traditional desktops.
3. VDI costs less than traditional desktops.

Now count the number of "true" answers you have.

0: Congratulations! You do know VDI. You have our permission to skip ahead.
1-2: Okay, so you know at least something about VDI, but it's probably a good idea to brush up, so we suggest that you do not skip ahead.
3: You work for Citrix or VMware. Keep reading.

The Promise of VDI

If you've been in the IT industry for awhile, you know that virtualization and hypervisors were first applied to servers. (Actually, if you've been in the industry for a really long time, you know virtualization first applied to mainframes, but that's not the same as what we're talking about here.)

In the early 2000s, VMware invented virtualization software for the x86-based servers that companies had installed by the rackful in their data centers. This virtualization software enabled companies to consolidate underutilized servers into fewer, higher-utilized servers. The benefits were immediate in terms of cost, power, and physical space savings.

Decoupling logical server virtual machines from the underlying physical hardware also enabled companies to get higher availability via new technologies like live migrations and instant snapshot-based backups.

In other words, server virtualization was a slam dunk, and within about five years (from about 2003 to 2008), we went from most people saying "I will never virtualize a production server" to "I have virtualized all of my production servers."

VMware was the driving force behind the x86 server virtualization movement, and in 2006, they started talking about the benefits of applying their server virtualization technologies to desktops. They called this virtual desktop infrastructure, or VDI. The idea was that instead of installing and running your Windows desktop locally on a cheap desktop computer, why not run a whole bunch of Windows desktops as virtual machines in your data center? The people pushing VDI (VMware in the early days, but eventually Citrix, Dell, HP, Cisco, and even Microsoft) claimed VDI had several benefits, including:

- VDI saves you money through a lower total cost of ownership. VDI desktops are easier to manage, which saves on costs, and the thin client devices that connect to the virtual desktops are more robust, use less electricity, and last longer than the desktops they're replacing.

- VDI offers better security, since no data is stored on the endpoint. The idea is that if someone steals a thin client or a laptop, there's nothing on it of value. All the sensitive data is in the data center with the desktop virtual machines.

- VDI means that users can work from anywhere, on any device. Since the desktop runs in the data center, users can instantly connect from wherever they are, including the office, a hotel, at home, or at Starbucks. They instantly have access to their Windows desktop in the exact state they left it in. Also, they can use any type of device, be it a thin client, a work computer, a personal MacBook, or an iPad.

- VDI means higher uptime, since a client device that has been dropped or has had coffee spilled on it can be swapped out instantly for a new one that picks up right where the last one left off. Also, since the desktops are in the data center, they're running on server-class hardware with formal change controls, so they're less likely to go down. When a server does have problems, the desktops can be live-migrated to a different server without impacting users.

- VDI means easier image management. Since all the VDI desktops run in the data center, you can centrally patch them via a reliable high-speed connection. Better yet, VDI technologies allow a single gold image to be used for multiple users, so you have to patch and maintain only a single image, which is instantly made available to hundreds or thousands of users the next time they log in.

- VDI means simpler provisioning because the VDI administrator can simply click a button to instantly provision the user's VDI desktop and login account. Then the user can log in and be productive immediately from whatever device he or she has at the moment. No waiting for manual application installs or laptop shipping.

- VDI means more consistent performance because users' desktops run on known server hardware with known performance characteristics. Even if a user's personal laptop is slow, the VDI desktop runs at full speed.
- VDI is virtualization, and you already know how to do virtualization. Since VDI is just desktops running on hypervisors in your data center, and you already have a bunch of virtual servers today, VDI is just a logical extension of that. Nothing more to learn!

The Reality of VDI

VDI sounds pretty amazing, doesn't it? We agree that, yeah, on paper it does sound good, but the reality of VDI leaves a lot to be desired. If you want proof of that, just look at the adoption rates of VDI we referenced in the last chapter: Today's rate of VDI adoption is somewhere in the 1% to 3% range for enterprise desktops. That statistic reveals all, because if VDI were really so awesome, everyone would be doing it! (Just like server virtualization, which went from 0% to 90% in five years all by itself!)

Where VDI Falls Short of Expectations

So why isn't VDI so awesome? What makes it so hard? We can boil it down to a few key points:

- A VDI desktop is not inherently easier to manage than a traditional, non-VDI desktop. So the automatic management benefit is a myth.
- A VDI desktop is not inherently more secure than a traditional, non-VDI desktop. So the automatic security benefit is a myth too.
- The user experience on a VDI desktop is not as good as that on a traditional laptop or desktop.

- Even though the claim is that VDI has lower TCO and is cheaper than traditional desktops, the reality is that when comparing apples to apples, VDI is more expensive than existing desktops.
- Designing, building, and tuning a VDI environment is hard.

We recognize that these are some fairly damning statements about VDI, so we're going to explore them in depth so you understand why we feel the way we do. And remember, since DaaS is just VDI that you pay someone else to host, you have to understand each of these points if you want to be successful with DaaS.

A VDI desktop is not easier to manage

Many people argue that VDI desktops are easier to manage than traditional desktops and laptops. If you ask them why, they say it's because with VDI, multiple users can share the same disk image. So if you have 100 users, managing one single disk image is much easier than managing 100 separate images, right?

Yes!

We totally agree with that! We agree that managing a single disk image is much easier than managing lots of individual ones. But does that mean that VDI is easier to manage? Not so fast!

Multiple users sharing an image is possible only if you lock down that image, since any changes a user makes are lost when he or she logs off or when you refresh the base image.

Of course not every user in your company uses the exact same application mix, so in order for multiple users to share the same image, you can install all of your applications for every user in your base image, but then all the users see all the apps. (There's a product from FSLogix that can hide apps on a per-user basis if you go this route.) Alternately you can use application virtualization or streaming software to customize which applications are streamed on demand to which users (like with App-V or ThinApp). Either option means that hundreds of users can share a single disk image, and going this route is probably easier to manage than dealing with hundreds of unique images for each user.

But here's the thing: If you go through all that, your management savings are coming from the fact that you are taking a Wild West "before" environment where any user can install anything and replacing it with a formal, well-designed, locked-down environment where users don't have the same freedoms. In other words, your savings aren't coming from VDI at all—they're coming from the fact that you're taking away your users' freedoms.

Easier to manage? Yes! Because of VDI? No!

If you just want to make your desktops easier to manage, why don't you just take away your users' rights on their existing traditional desktop PCs? App virtualization, layering, and user lockdown all work well on traditional desktops and can make them easier to manage. You don't need VDI to do that at all!

Next, people say, "Okay, so forget that disk image sharing thing. Even if you go with one-to-one 'personal' disk images, VDI is easier to manage because all the desktops are running in the data center and therefore 'closer' to the administrator."

True, but man, it's a bit of a stretch if you're using *that* as a justification for VDI.

A VDI desktop is not more secure

Another reality of VDI is that while many people sell VDI as being more secure, it's our belief that VDI desktops are *not* inherently more secure than traditional desktops and laptops. This is a highly controversial position, but we strongly believe it.

To be fair, we believe that VDI *can* be used to deliver the most secure Windows desktops in the world, so it's true that using VDI can improve the security of your desktop environment. But there's a big caveat to that: In order to realize those security improvements, you have to make a lot of changes to the way you manage and secure your Windows desktops when moving to VDI. In other words, the mere act of moving your desktops to VDI *does not make them more secure*. In fact, if you simply replicate your existing desktop environment into a VDI environment without making any changes, we'd argue that that's actually *less* secure than your old environment.

We have several reasons for feeling this way.

First, the basic supporting argument of the "VDI is more secure" movement is that with VDI, your desktops and all their data are locked in your data center. So if a user loses a client device or you have a burglary at your office, those client devices don't have any data on them. Fair enough.

The problem we have with that line of reasoning is that if you're equating a stolen laptop with data loss, that means you're worried about the data at rest. If so, you can easily address that vulnerability with disk encryption. (When we say that, we're not talking about sending an email out to all your users encouraging them to install some security product. We're talking about enterprise-grade disk encryption products from vendors like Symantec, Sophos, Druva, or McAfee. These products can guarantee that your laptop disks are encrypted. They include centralized management consoles and the ability to restrict the laptop's ability to boot or wake up if it doesn't download a centralized decryption key.)

For years we've been talking about these products as alternatives to VDI if all you're concerned about is data loss. But the number of people who just don't get it still amazes us. Someone once said, "Wait, if my newly encrypted laptops need to connect to my servers in order to get the decryption keys to boot up, that means if the user doesn't have a network connection or if my server goes down, the users can't work!" That's true. But, come on, we're talking about VDI versus enterprise laptop encryption here. If your argument is that VDI is better than laptop encryption, the same connectivity limitations apply with VDI. If you're using VDI, your users *also* can't work without a network connection or if your servers go down.

So if your main security concern is data loss from a stolen laptop, these enterprise disk encryption products are a heck of a lot cheaper and easier to implement than VDI, and they don't bring the other downsides of VDI with them.

But honestly all this talk about disk encryption is just a sideshow to the *real* Windows desktop security challenge, which is that a Microsoft Windows desktop is not a secure operating environment. Windows desktops are vulnerable to who-knows-what zero-day exploits and malware and viruses and Trojans and keyboard sniffers and all those types of things. *Those* are the real security problems with Windows—not stolen laptops—and unfortunate-ly, all of the real bad unknown Windows things are just as much of a risk in VDI environments as they are when Windows is running on a laptop or desktop PC.

The good news is that the IT security industry has tools and techniques to deal with many of these *actual* security issues, and it's imperative that you have a plan for them. But what's important is that you have this plan regardless of whether your users are run-ning their Windows desktops the traditional way or as VDI virtual machines in your data center. In other words, your VDI desktops still have to have antivirus and browser protections and malware-fighting tools.

Now, again, as we said in the beginning part of this section, it *is* possible to design your VDI environment so that it's more secure than your traditionally deployed laptops. After all, since your VDI desktops run in your data center, you can have security software that analyzes every network connection going in and out of every desktop without exception. Also, with VDI there is no chance that a user is doing something crazy when he or she is disconnected, since there's no such thing as being disconnected. With VDI you can guarantee that every desktop has the latest patches and secu-rity updates and that the desktops meet your current best prac-tices and standards—and you can block access to ones that don't. With VDI you can easily implement two-factor authentication at your gateway and know for sure that no users can get around it. With VDI you can control whether users are able to download files, use USB peripherals, or even copy and paste from their VDI desk-top to their client device.

The bottom line is that with VDI, all of your desktops are running in your data center, which is totally under your control, so you absolutely have the opportunity to run a highly secure en-vironment. But doing so requires an intentional security design—it's far from an automatic benefit you get with VDI, and it's some-thing that's often not included in the cost and ROI models that people use to calculate the costs and benefits of their VDI.

The VDI desktop has a worse user experience

Even though today's VDI products have made huge strides toward improving the user experience, the reality is that VDI desktops run in the data center while users are out in the world. Putting a network between users and their desktops creates challenges, including performance issues, peripheral complexities, and users' inability to work if there's no internet connection. Taken together, these factors mean that often the user experience on VDI desktops is worse than that on even a low-end PC or laptop.

The core problem stems from the fact that so many people try to use cost savings as a way to justify moving to VDI. (More on that in the next section.) In your pre-VDI PC and laptop world, each user has a multi-gigahertz processor with a couple of CPU cores, a GPU, 2GB-plus of RAM, a hard disk with 50-plus IOPS, USB with 480 Mbps bandwidth, and a display (or two!) running at 1900×1200 resolution with 32-bit color updating 30 times per second.

Compare that with what you get with VDI, where you end up putting multiple users on a CPU core (so each user gets *less* than a full core), there's typically no GPU, memory is oversubscribed, USB bandwidth is limited to the network speed, and the display does its best to keep up but drops frames or pixels every time things start to back up.

Of course these limitations aren't new with VDI. We've known about them since the Terminal Server/Remote Desktop Session Host/Citrix days of the 1990s and 2000s. The difference back then was that most Terminal Server or Citrix environments were used to deliver only a few critical applications here and there, and in most cases they were business apps that didn't have high graphical elements.

But VDI is different. VDI is not just a few apps, but a whole freaking desktop, with every app the user needs! (After all, if you can't do every app in the VDI environment, that means you have some apps running locally on users' traditional PCs or laptops, which in turn means you're managing *two* desktops for each user. If that's the case, we ask, "Why are you doing VDI? Why bother?")

The good news is that many of these graphical limitations can be addressed. AMD and Nvidia have GPU cards that plug into VDI servers to give users access to GPUs. You can increase the bandwidth at your remote offices to provide more room for more pixels and more screens. You can buy client devices that are capable of supporting graphics, video, and webcams. You can use solutions like Dropbox to share files instead of leveraging USB sticks.

But each of these things costs money, and many of them are not in the initial plans and cost models that companies build to justify their VDI projects. In fact, since many people (erroneously) think VDI is about saving money, they actually *cut* resources from their VDI users in order to make their cost models look better. (Oops!) While this will make your CIO happy, it has the opposite effect on your users, who now have to deal with being crammed onto a single CPU core with six other people, no GPU, no video support, and only 20 IOPS.

When it comes to user experience, there's good VDI and bad VDI. We've all experienced both, and we know that good VDI costs a lot more than bad VDI (both in terms of server hardware and bandwidth). The question is this: If you put your VDI environment next to a traditional desktop PC and hide the wires, would your users prefer the VDI or the traditional desktop? If they choose the traditional desktop, then guess what? Your VDI is giving a worse user experience! So now you have to decide whether you're okay with that or you're willing to spend the extra money to improve the quality of the VDI user experience to match what your users have grown accustomed to with their traditional PCs.

As a quick side note, some companies use "non-traditional" metrics to define the quality of a user's experience. For example, they say, "Okay, so VDI isn't going to look as pretty as the desktop PCs we're replacing. But the VDI *does* have additional benefits for the user, such as the ability to log in and pick up right where they left off as they bounce between the office, their home, and their tablet. That has value and increases their happiness with their user experience."

Another approach some companies take is to give users options to get their "good experience" from outside their VDI desktop. For example, if your VDI can't support YouTube and webcams, maybe you buy your users iPads for web browsing and Facebook and all the other things your VDI can't do. Sure, it sounds crazy at first, but think about it: What does an iPad cost? $400? Compare that with how much more you'd have to spend—per user—to add servers, bandwidth, and GPUs to enable them to do all that via your VDI. Suddenly $400 per user doesn't seem like that bad of a deal!

In fact, we've seen companies use this iPad trick to get their users to give up their admin rights on their Windows desktops too. It's a win-win! IT has better control, since users aren't installing God knows what on their desktop PCs, and users are happy because they can use YouTube, Angry Birds, and Facebook on their iPads. Plus, your users will think they work for a cool company because they all have iPads now.

The bottom line is that while it's certainly possible to provide an amazing desktop computing experience via VDI, if you just take the same dollars you've been spending to buy those low-end PCs all these years and funnel it into your VDI project, you're going to end up with a user experience that is worse than what you had before. We're not saying that's a bad thing, but we're just pointing it out because a lot of people don't consider this when they think about all the cool reasons they want to use VDI.

A VDI desktop is not cheaper

Here's the mother of all misconceptions around VDI: People think that a VDI desktop is cheaper than a traditional desktop, but when you compare apples to apples, it's not. In other words, VDI is more expensive than traditional PCs and laptops. (Another way to phrase this is that a VDI desktop can cost the same thing as a traditional desktop but with a lower quality of experience.)

We could write an entire book about this. Actually, we almost did, as our book "The New VDI Reality" has an entire 4,400-word chapter called "VDI Costs & Myths." But since you're reading this book and not that one, we'll try to summarize it here.

First, when talking about the costs of VDI, the first thing we like to point out is that while it's true that a VDI desktop is more expensive than a traditional one, *that's okay!* A VDI desktop has more features than a traditional desktop, so spending more money to get more features is fine. That's how the world works!

Of course we've been saying this for years—and people have been challenging us on this for years—but we still stand behind our view that VDI desktops cost more than traditional ones. While explaining this concept at an event a few years ago, one of the attendees claimed that for his company, VDI was actually cheaper. He explained that at that moment they were spending $1,000 per desktop for new PCs every four years. If they went to VDI, they could buy $200 thin clients instead of $1,000 desktops. Then the company could use some of the $800 saved per desktop to buy the back-end servers, storage, licenses, etc., for the complete environment, which he estimated at $500 per user. All in all, he explained, the company could save $300 per desktop by going to VDI.

At first you might think, "Okay, so for this guy, VDI is about saving money." But there are actually several problems with this example, and it turns out his alleged savings are total garbage!

First, while this guy was spending $1,000 for each new desktop, you can buy desktops for $300. So we would suggest that the best way for this guy to save money is to stop buying $1,000 PCs and instead buy $300 ones. Now, he might argue that he actually needs $1,000 desktops. Maybe his users are power users and actually need that much computer. Okay, fine. But if that's the case, there's no way that a $200 thin client powered by a $500 back-end VDI kit is going to come anywhere close to delivering the computing power and user experience he needs!

So in this guy's case, is he saving money with his new plan? Yes! But is he saving money because he's going to VDI? No! He's saving money because he's drastically cutting down the amount of desktop computing that he's delivering to his users. He's saving money by delivering a lesser user experience. If this is fine for his users, that not only means that he has been spending way too much on his $1,000 PCs, but also that the baseline should be $300 per user. If VDI is costing him $800 per user, that means VDI is still the more expensive solution. Sure, he's saving money, but only because he was overpaying for PCs by so much that VDI still works out to be cheaper than the old way.

We already talked about how sometimes people say, "VDI will be cheaper for us because we're going to have shared (and therefore locked-down) disk images, which means that users can't screw things up and that will be easier to manage than the current Wild West world of personal images." Again, that's true. Locked-down desktops *are* cheaper than non-locked-down desktops. But again, that money savings comes from the fact that they're locking down their desktop images, not because they're using VDI. And again, if you just want to save money, simply lock down your existing physical desktops and skip VDI altogether!

To be clear, there are many wonderful and perfectly valid reasons to use VDI. It's just that saving money is not one of them. And if you use VDI as your excuse to completely overhaul the way you deliver desktops, it's the complete overhaul that's saving you money, not the actual VDI.

The root of the problem of course is that most people build cost models to "prove" to themselves or their bosses how much money they can save by going to VDI. The problem with cost models is that you can make them show whatever you want, especially when it comes to soft costs. For more details, google [how to lie with cost models] to find an article we wrote showing all the nefarious ways to manipulate them, or check out either of our VDI books to find out eleven specific ways people lie with cost models.

All that said, trying to save money with VDI is like trying to increase security with VDI—it's possible but not automatic. So while you don't automatically get cost savings just by going to VDI, we certainly believe that there's excess fat in most people's desktop environments that can be cut, and if you're rethinking your desktop environment from scratch at the same time you move to VDI, it's possible to end up with a lower-cost environment post-VDI than what you had going in. That's totally fine, and we support it. Just be aware that you're getting your cost savings because of those other changes you made, not because you're moving to VDI.

VDI is hard

The final challenge of VDI that causes it to fall short of many people's expectations is the simple fact that building VDI is hard. Enterprise IT shops have, what, twenty years of experience building, deploying, managing, and maintaining desktop PCs and laptops? VDI is a brand new way of doing all of that—especially if you're also trying to move to a locked-down shared desktop or increase the overall security of your desktop environment.

This challenge is exacerbated by the fact that server virtualization was an enormous success for most companies, causing people to think, "Hey, since I virtualized all these servers, virtualizing a bunch of desktops should be easy, right?" We sympathize with where they're coming from, especially since most IT pros graduate from desktops to servers in their careers, leading many to the unfortunate supposition that servers must be harder. (Seriously, we've even heard people at VMware say it: VDI is *just* desktops, so how hard can it be?)

The problem is that, across the board, server virtualization couldn't be more different than desktop virtualization. The reason virtualization took off originally was because companies had all these physical servers in one room (the data center) that were all running at about 20% utilization. So consolidating those under-utilized servers with virtualization made sense. When it came to desktops, people thought, "Hey, look at what virtualization did to our servers! Let's get that for our desktops too!"

While that was a nice thought, the key difference is that servers were already in the data center to begin with, so consolidating them meant that each server instance just moved a few shelves over once it became a VM. But for desktops, they had to be moved from out in the wild (near the user) into the data center (far away from the user), and that's just not the same thing.

The other big difference is that virtualizing a server starts with something you already know: how busy that server is in the data center. It's easy to be confident in consolidating those servers because the users aren't going to change how they use the server after they've been virtualized. But when it comes to desktops, how do you know how busy your users are? Do you have utilization data on the CPU, memory, processes, and Windows applications that your users use in your pre-VDI environment? Do you know how much time they spend actually using their desktops versus the time the desktop is on but idle? Do you know how many users open their laptops at night and whether they all do it at once? If you don't know this, how can you even begin to design a VDI server? Are you just totally guessing?

Still another difference between virtualizing a server and a desktop is that users intimately interact with the UI of their desktop—something they don't do on servers. For example, if your virtual Exchange Server is running slow and adding half a second to each message that comes in, no one would complain or even notice. But in the desktop world, if there's a half-second or even a quarter-second lag between the time the user clicks on the Start button and the time the Start menu appears, you'll hear about it!

The final big difference between server virtualization and desktop virtualization is that users plug all sorts of different peripherals into their desktops. In a traditional desktop environment, a user can plug in a USB drive or camera and it will work fine. In a VDI desktop environment, if users plug a device into their client, their copy of Windows that's running in the data center has to connect via a USB over the network to access that device. What will that experience be like if the webcam driver tries to reserve 100 Mbps on the virtual USB bus that you're redirecting over your network?

Of course these issues are just the tip of the iceberg. How are you going to handle printing, logging in, security, performance management, and the dozens and dozens of other issues around VDI? Trust us, building VDI is hard!

Of course you might already know this and are thinking, "Umm, yeah, I get that. That's why I'm reading a book about DaaS. I want VDI without the hard part!" Good point! So while this chapter was focused on people's expectations and the reality of VDI, the next chapter will look at where VDI has worked well and how people can be successful with it. *Then*, finally, we'll be ready to talk about DaaS.

3. How to Succeed with VDI

After reading the last chapter, which focused on how VDI fails to live up to people's unrealistic expectations, you might think that we're not fans of VDI. Actually, the opposite is true. After all, we've dedicated our careers to VDI, and we've written multiple books and thousands of articles about it, so trust us—we love VDI!

What we don't love is when people try to use VDI where it doesn't make sense, since in those cases, VDI fails and leaves people with a bad opinion of it.

Instead, being successful with VDI means:

1. Understanding where VDI is awesome and where it makes sense.
2. Building VDI in a way that can work where it makes sense.

These two steps may seem almost insultingly obvious, but unfortunately most people don't think about them when it comes to VDI, which is why we have so many failed VDI projects in the world.

So in this chapter we're going to address these two things to ensure you know how to be successful with VDI. After that we'll move on to talk about DaaS.

Advantages of VDI

Like we've said again and again, VDI is great *if* you use it where it makes sense. In our minds, use cases can be grouped into five categories:

- User flexibility
- Device independence
- Centralized management
- Consistent performance
- Possibly increased security

VDI means user flexibility

Since VDI desktops run on servers in data centers, users can connect to them from anywhere. This means it's just as easy for users to connect to their desktops from the office as it is from their home, a friend's house, or wherever else they happen to be.

What's even better about this is that with VDI, desktops can stay running all the time. So when users move to a new location, they don't have to power up their laptop, open all the applications, open their files, and get all their Windows arranged before they can start working again. Instead, when they disconnect from their VDI session, everything stays running on the server exactly as they left it. They could start typing an email in the office, jump in the car to drive home, and when they connect again hours later, pick up exactly where they left off, with the blinking cursor still sitting in the middle of the email message they were writing.

This is awesome from a user's point of view. A VDI desktop is like a personal Windows environment that never has to be powered down and is accessible from anywhere.

VDI means device independence

Another huge benefit of VDI—for both you and the user—is that the same well-managed VDI desktop is consistently delivered to users regardless of the client device they're using.

This is great for you because it means you don't have to worry about the client device users are connecting from. If they want to use a Mac, that's fine! If they have a home computer, you don't have to do anything to it or support it. If they can get to the web, they can get to your VDI. (And if they can't get to the web, that's not your problem!) If your users are remote workers, contractors, or employees of a newly acquired company, you don't have to care about what kind of computers they have or how they're hooked up. You just give them the address of your VDI environment and they're instantly productive.

This is also great for users, since they can now use whatever device they want. Again, big laptop, old desktop, new small Mac—it doesn't matter because they're all the same when it comes to VDI.

What's more, users love VDI because they can combine this device-independence advantage with the user-flexibility advantage, using VDI to bounce between devices and locations. Sure, a tablet or phone might not be the most appropriate device to use to connect to a Windows desktop, but with VDI, the user at least has the *option* for occasional or emergency purposes. And sure, a user might not plan to work at night, but it's nice to know that they can power on any internet-connected device on the planet and have instant access to their entire Windows environment, including all their apps and files.

At the end of the day, if you use VDI, you only have to worry about the actual Windows desktop itself. Your days of managing the client devices are over.

VDI means centralized management

Another advantage of VDI is that all of your users' desktops run in your data center, so it's easy to keep them up to date. We're not talking about that non-persistent image sharing thing we mentioned in the first chapter. We're talking about the fact that all the desktops you need to manage—even if they're all different from each other—are running on nice, fast hardware inside your data center.

Having your desktops run in your data center makes them easier to manage in every way. When you push out patches, you know they'll get to the desktops quickly. Since all of your desktops are virtual machines, you know that you can power on a desktop whenever you need to get your updates installed. And with VDI, if anything weird is happening on a desktop, you know that you can connect to it to fix it.

Oh, and of course you don't care about end-user hardware anymore, so the days of slow laptops and failing desktop hard drives gumming up your works are over!

Compare all that with the traditional distributed desktop PC model, where patches and updates have to download and machines have to be powered on in order to receive them. It seems like traditional desktop engineers spend more time trying to pin down remote users than they do actually managing desktops!

VDI means consistent performance

One other great thing about VDI is that the performance of the Windows desktop is decoupled from the speed of the client device or the network connection. This is a big deal for desktop support folks! Both of us authors began our IT careers by working on help desks, and we've shared stories over beers of the crazy home computers that people used to bring in back when we had to configure their VPN or Outlook settings. Talk about crapware-laden pieces of garbage! (The computers, not the users. We have loved and will continue to love every user we've ever worked with.)

And then there's the traditional advantage of server-based computing: When your desktop runs in the data center, it has a full-speed connection back to all the application servers. All your client/server apps, your network shares, and your email just scream when the desktop is running on high-quality server hardware inside the data center.

VDI can lead to increased desktop security

If you read the previous chapter, you know we spent a lot of time talking (ranting?) about how moving to VDI doesn't automatically mean that your desktops are more secure. In fact, we wrote that in a lot of cases the *opposite* is true. That's because people think they're getting better security with VDI and let their guard down, when in reality the real desktop security issues today have to do with Windows and users, and you have the same Windows with the same users regardless of whether you're using VDI or not.

That said, we do acknowledge that it *can* be possible for you to design a VDI environment that's more secure than a traditional desktop environment. The reason for this again comes back to control. If your desktop computers are running in your data center, they're always in your zone of control. You can know 100% what network traffic is going in and out. You can be 100% certain that your security suite is running, scanning for threats, malware, and viruses. You can use your virtualization architecture to run your security tools "underneath" the VMs, giving you confidence that there's nothing a user can do to get around them. If you're worried about rogue users, using VDI means you can audit or screen-record everything the users do.

In other words, your users have to do all their work on VMs running in your data center. Since they can't work while disconnected, there's no chance that they can do anything that isn't under your control.

Notice that when we talk about desktop security, we didn't bring up the fact that with VDI, no data is on the endpoint. As we said in the previous chapter, we believe that if a lost or stolen laptop is your biggest concern, implementing enterprise disk encryption software is much cheaper and easier than using VDI. In other words, don't turn to VDI just to address the threat of lost laptops.

That said, it is true that with VDI, no data is on the endpoint. So if you're going to VDI for other reasons but you also want to increase the security of your environment, a nice side benefit of VDI is that you get the enhanced security of not having data on the endpoint.

So considering all this, we will agree that yes, it's *possible* to use VDI to increase the security of your desktop computing environment, as long as you figure out how to address all the malware, virus, and zero-day vulnerabilities out there.

How to Succeed with VDI

The last section was all about the scenarios in which VDI is awesome. Now we want to talk about how you can succeed with VDI. Obviously, we could just say, "Do not do the things we talked about in Chapter 2, and use VDI only to gain the benefits we just listed above." Actually, yeah, we're going to say that exactly. That's how you succeed.

We'll just tweak that by adding in a few things we haven't discussed yet. If you want to succeed with VDI in your environment, keep the following things in mind:

- VDI is just a form factor.
- VDI should be an option for some, not a mandate for all.
- VDI can solve certain problems. If you try to solve those problems, it will be good. If you try to solve other problems, it will not be good.

Let's take a deeper look into each of these points.

Understand that VDI is just a form factor

A lot of people throw around phrases like *big deal*, *game changing*, and *transformational* when describing VDI. But in reality, VDI is not (and should not be) a big deal. VDI is not game changing. In fact, VDI is nothing more than a form factor change. It's the same Windows desktop you've always had, just delivered in a different shape. Once you understand how *not* a big deal VDI is, you'll actually be able to be more successful with VDI.

In order to appreciate this, let's take a step back. The desktop PC world began with, well, desktop PCs! They plugged into the wall, and you couldn't move them easily. That was fine for a while. Then laptops came out. Laptops had some "game-changing" features in their day, like you could take them with you and work from your hotel or home, and they didn't have to be plugged into the wall in order for you to turn them on. Of course laptops had downsides too, like the fact that they were more expensive than desktops but less powerful and with smaller screens.

So we had desktops and laptops. Back then, everyone understood this. Enterprises bought desktops for some users and laptops for others. Note that they did not run out and buy laptops for everyone, as that would have been irrational. They just bought laptops where they made sense.

The key is that laptops did *not* change the way companies managed or delivered Windows. Companies didn't have laptop strategies and desktop strategies—they had Windows strategies.

Sure, some companies might have used the timing of their laptop rollout to also upgrade the version of Windows or Office they used or implement some kind of automatic software distribution tool. But those changes were a matter of timing convenience, not a major change brought on by laptops. Everything else—what versions of Windows they ran, how they did patching, antivirus platforms, application installs, etc.—was the same across both laptops and desktops, both before and after the rollout.

This also applies to VDI. We already talked about how a lot of people fail with VDI because they try to change too much at once, such as moving users to shared locked-down images and implementing application and user virtualization at the same time they're moving to VDI. Instead, if you want to be successful with VDI, understand that VDI is nothing more than a form factor change. Just like laptops provided more—some would say "game changing"—features than desktop computers, VDI desktops provide more features than laptops or desktops. But that doesn't mean you should freak out and try to change your whole world just because you go to VDI.

What's more, it doesn't mean you need to create a VDI strategy. Seriously, we know it sounds crazy, but creating a VDI strategy is no more necessary than creating a laptop strategy! Sure, you need to understand which VDI product you'll use and how it will work, but companies should be staying the course with their Windows desktop strategies and understand that when you deploy a Windows desktop to a user, you now have options for a desktop PC, a laptop, or a VDI virtual machine.

VDI should be an option for some, not a mandate for all

Building on the understanding that VDI is just a form factor, the next key to succeeding with an implementation is to understand that VDI is not right for everyone. Just like we didn't force all of our users to switch to laptops back in 1997, we shouldn't switch all of our users to VDI just because it's now an option.

Our favorite example of this is a story from VMware a few years ago. At one of their conferences, the company did a case study on their own internal VDI deployment to 3,000 users. Of course Citrix, being a huge competitor of VMware, jumped on Twitter, saying something like, "VMware has 11,000 employees, but only 3,000 of them are using VDI. That proves that VMware's VDI sucks, because even they can't make it work for all their users!" In actuality, this was nothing more than competitor mudslinging because VMware's implementation of VDI was exactly how it should be. It's not that VMware's VDI product was so bad that they couldn't deploy it to all of their users, rather, it's that VMware was smart and deployed VDI only to the subset of users where it made sense. If only every VDI deployment was like this!

To succeed with VDI, look for the users and use cases where it makes sense and use it only in those cases. If that means you're using VDI for only 2% of your users, then so be it! Those 2% will be happy to be using VDI, and the other 98% will be happy they're not.

Use VDI to solve the problems that VDI can solve

Given everything we've covered so far about the myths of VDI, it's easy to understand how VDI gets forced into scenarios where it doesn't make sense. If a CIO is sold on the VDI concept with promises that it will make the company's desktops more manageable, more secure, and less expensive, then *of course* that CIO will try to use VDI for as many users as possible!

But doing so means that it would be used in a vast number of inappropriate cases, ultimately leading people to shout "VDI sucks" instead of the more nuanced "VDI is good for some and bad for others," as we mentioned in the previous section.

So if you want to succeed with VDI, use it to solve the problems that VDI can solve (as we outlined in our "Why VDI is awesome" section). Use VDI to enable users to be more flexible and work from anywhere. Use it for offices where you don't have onsite support staff or where you don't control the devices your users will use. Don't use VDI to save money or to make your environment more manageable.

Now that you have a decent foundation of what VDI is and isn't, and where it works and doesn't work, we can finally dig into the details of that flavor of VDI we call DaaS.

4. Bringing in DaaS

Now that we're all caught up on where VDI works, where it doesn't, and how to be successful with it, we can finally start looking at DaaS itself. We've already said several times that DaaS is just VDI that you pay someone else to operate. That means that from a technical standpoint, DaaS and VDI are basically the same thing. In both cases we're taking the desktops from your users' cubicles and placing them in a data center somewhere.

As you dig deeper, the similarities between DaaS and VDI continue. Both have the same protocols, and both share similar back-end components like virtualization host servers, connection brokers, a web interface for the users to connect to, client software, storage optimization, and so on.

Of course there are some differences between DaaS and VDI too. Since DaaS providers are 100% dedicated to hosting services for multiple customers, a lot of orchestration and isolation components are needed to protect their customers from each other, bring new customers on board, and shift around workloads that you wouldn't have if you built VDI yourself. (These extra DaaS-specific things are transparent to you and your end users though.)

None of this takes away from the fact that the *main* difference between DaaS and VDI is that DaaS is just a business arrangement. It's just like paying someone else to mow your lawn. Sure, you could use your own mower and do it yourself, or you could hire someone who knows exactly what they're doing, owns a better mower, and can do it faster. Either way though, you get your grass cut.

Many people claim that DaaS is VDI without the work. If your VDI project is stuck thanks to some technical, financial, or political snag, wouldn't you like to just punt it over to someone else to finish? (That sounds good to us!) As one person we interviewed put it, DaaS closes out all those failed VDI experiments that everyone tried over the past eight years.

On the other hand, choosing DaaS puts the pressure on, since paying someone else means there's no more blaming the infrastructure, cost, politics, or anything else if your project fails. If you were doing VDI yourself and the implementation didn't go well, you could always blame it on VDI being too hard, having poor performance, or being too expensive. But once you decide to go to DaaS, you have to take all those past excuses off the table.

The final point we'll make about DaaS is something we've said a few times already but that's important enough to mention again: DaaS is about running Windows desktops in a data center, so all the same pros and cons of doing that with VDI apply to DaaS. If you looked at your desktops and decided they're not a good fit for VDI, they're also not going to be a good fit for DaaS. And all that stuff about how it's important to use VDI only where it makes sense and to not force everyone to use it applies to DaaS too.

Is DaaS the Same Thing as Cloud?

The sad truth is that a lot of people are excited about DaaS simply because DaaS involves the cloud. It's like this decade's version of desktop virtualization. You take desktops (which are boring) and move them to the cloud (which is exciting). So DaaS makes desktops exciting!

This is often something the people you work for think about. They'll come up to you and say, "Hey, that cloud thing is about saving money or being modern or whatever, so we need to move everything to the cloud!"

So the real question here is, "Is a DaaS desktop the same thing as a cloud desktop?" Or, "If my boss says we have to move to the cloud, does DaaS count?" The answer, quite fortunately, is whatever you want it to be. If you want DaaS to be the cloud, then yeah, we'll call it the cloud. If you want to do DaaS but your boss hates the cloud, fine, we'll just call it "outsourced VDI" instead. Really it doesn't matter because these are all just BS terms that mean nothing.

The issue is that there's no single agreed upon definition of the cloud. Paying a monthly fee to access your desktops from an outsourced Citrix provider has been going on for almost twenty years. Remember those "application service providers" that were all the rage at Citrix iForum 2001? Weren't those the exact same thing as DaaS? So what's the difference between DaaS of 2014 and the outsourced Citrix desktops of 1998, apart from the trendiness of the terms?

Obviously there is no *real* difference. We simply define DaaS as a business arrangement in which you pay someone else to host your desktops. Does the provider have to host them in the cloud for it to count as DaaS? No? Yes? Who cares? What does that even mean? All that should matter to you is that you can get access to Microsoft Windows desktops from your DaaS provider. How the provider does it on the back-end shouldn't matter at all.

The same applies to VDI you build yourself. Now there's this thing called private cloud, which as far as we can tell is just a fancy rebranding of the term "on-premises data center." Yeah, yeah, we know that VMware wants to call these data centers private clouds because they have all sorts of virtualization and automation and connections to public clouds and stuff, but come on, isn't that what all IT is about these days? (And really, again, who cares?)

The point here is that we're starting to hear people talk about things like internal DaaS, private DaaS and on-premises DaaS—all of which are just fancy names for VDI. But again, in terms of what you call it, we don't care. If you want to call your VDI something like private cloud DaaS just because your boss is into that kind of thing, go for it! What you call the technology doesn't make a darn bit of difference in terms of how it works.

DaaS Fits into the Evolution of IT

One last thing that's worth exploring is if you look at the evolution of IT over the past decade, the concept of DaaS fits in nicely and makes a lot of sense. Even we acknowledge that.

Companies have been outsourcing certain elements of IT for a long time. Even though not too many companies have outsourced their VDI yet, a lot of companies—even huge publicly traded ones—have started to outsource the "easier" things. For example, CRM systems are going to Salesforce, expense reporting and travel scheduling are going to Concur, and shipping and logistics are going to UPS.

Over time, companies have continued to warm up to the idea of placing their services outside their own data center walls. While it started with simple web-based SaaS applications, gradually companies are moving more fundamental aspects of their IT operations to the cloud. Many have now placed their email in the hands of Google or Microsoft, eschewing internal Exchange servers and all the complexities around running their own email systems (hardware, platforms, clients, antispam, antivirus, web access, gateways, replication, mailboxes, etc.) in favor of paying a few dollars a month per user.

Now we're starting to see IaaS and PaaS (Infrastructure as a Service and Platform as a Service) adoption as companies continue to move servers, storage, databases, and applications into the cloud. In many ways, DaaS is just a logical next step.

A lot has come together for DaaS to shine now. In the past, desktops weren't on the cloud list for the same reasons VDI didn't catch on. Since VDI was expensive and complicated, and the end result was usually a significantly reduced user experience compared with running local desktops, cloud providers didn't have much to offer in terms of benefits. Plus, we'd been deploying desktops the same way for nearly twenty years, and we knew the old way was efficient and cheap.

As technology matured, though, the concept of putting desktops in the cloud became more viable. Infrastructure technology improvements the providers needed to increase density came down in price, and other improvements like storage optimizations, advanced protocols, and graphics processing have addressed the user experience limitations.

All this adds up to DaaS becoming a viable option for outsourcing your desktops, and for many companies that have already embraced the cloud for some services, DaaS can be the next logical step. Amazon Web Services is a great example. Amazon's entry into the DaaS market with their WorkSpaces offering adds another service to the hundreds they currently offer, so for companies that are "going Amazon" for more and more of their IT services, the desktop is just another thing they can add to the list.

The challenge with desktops is that they aren't single applications you can provide access to from anywhere. Desktops are aggregation points for more applications and services. So if all your applications are in the cloud already, you don't need to put Windows there. Of course from an enterprise standpoint, there are lots of Windows applications that can't be converted to web-based or SaaS apps, which really is the attraction of DaaS in the first place.

So with that, let's take the new few chapters to look at the advantages and challenges of DaaS and moving your legacy Windows applications to the cloud. Then we'll dig into what you need to know to actually design your DaaS environment.

5. Advantages of DaaS

Let's take a quick look back at what we've established so far in this book. We talked about how DaaS is just VDI that you pay someone else for. We covered the myths and realities of VDI, as well as how you can be successful with it. And finally, we introduced the concept of DaaS and discussed how DaaS can be used to move your legacy Windows desktops and applications to the cloud.

So now let's get into the meat of this book. In this chapter, we're going to look at the advantages of DaaS. What's important here is that we're not going to cover the advantages of VDI, since we covered that back in Chapter 3. Rather, we're going to cover the additional advantages of VDI you get when you pay someone else to host it in a DaaS form.

We believe the further advantages DaaS has over VDI are:

- You don't have to know how to build or run VDI.
- There are no super-expensive up-front startup costs.
- Migration times are faster.

- Scaling is incremental.
- The costs of DaaS are known.
- DaaS is easy to test and pilot.
- DaaS providers have a better relationship with vendors than you.
- DaaS can have real savings with extended device lifecycles.
- DaaS environments are most likely cheaper, more secure, and more reliable than what you could build on your own.

Let's take a look at each of these.

You don't have to know how to run VDI

We covered this a bit already, but it's worth reinforcing. Since DaaS is the same thing as VDI except you're paying someone else to manage it, DaaS provides a nice VDI environment without you having to design, build, tune, or operate it. Remember, we've written a bunch of articles and books on VDI, so you can flip through those for more details about all the stuff you get to skip if you use DaaS. Here's a quick rundown:

- You don't need someone who knows all about VDI storage. You don't have to know what block-level single instance versus in-line deduping is. You don't have to know how to maximize the IOPS per desktop.
- You don't have to read white papers about which hypervisor is best or techniques for enabling performance caching.
- You don't need to sell the remote access concept to you security team.
- You don't need to coordinate lots of other IT resources and bribe them with pizza and beer to agree with you.

- You don't have to have deep technical knowledge of the VDI platform. Actually, you don't even have to decide between VDI platforms!
- The as yet undiscovered intricacies of the infrastructure can remain just that—undiscovered!
- You don't have to worry about scale, bottlenecks, or building out for high availability.

DaaS means no huge startup costs

A lot of people say "no capex" when they talk about the advantages of DaaS. (Capex is short for capital expenditures, which refers to the initial one-time costs for something. It's usually used in conjunction with opex, or operational expenditures, which are the recurring expenses associated with something.) So with DaaS, there's no capex because you don't have to buy huge amounts of hardware and licenses up front.

Compare that with traditional VDI, where you might have to spend tens or hundreds of thousands of dollars on server hardware, storage, and VDI product licenses—all before you bring a single user into production. With DaaS, that's all stuff the provider has invested in ahead of time, so you don't have to worry about it. (Not that there aren't any migration costs, but they pale in comparison to what it would cost to design and build your own VDI. We'll look at that later.)

Migrations are faster

When you use DaaS, you're paying for VDI on someone else's platform, which is already up and running. Compare that with how long it would take you to evaluate, design, buy, build, test, buy more, learn about, test, design, fix, and deploy.

Seriously, it can take months and months of work and thousands of work hours to design VDI to be used internally. When you choose DaaS, the core design is done. You cut literally months out of your migration project when you choose DaaS versus designing VDI yourself.

Scaling is incremental (and instant)

When you run your own VDI environment, you have to plan not only for the number of users you have, but also for future growth and excess capacity to handle outages. All this means your over-building your VDI and spending money on unused resources. Then whenever you want to add a few users, you have to go through this whole exercise again!

It's even worse when you need to add a few users when the environment is operating at 100% net efficiency (with the appropriate balance of consumed and redundant resources). You can't just shoehorn new users into your current environment because that would throw off the balance. Instead, you have to buy more hardware and software, plus spend time configuring it all, just for a few users. If you have to add additional servers or storage capacity, you could be forced to spend thousands or even tens of thousands of dollars, all to add capacity for just a few users.

Compare that with using DaaS, where you can incrementally scale your environment up one user at a time. Figuring out how to make that happen is up to the provider. (After all, that's what you're paying for!) Whether it's three people or 300, your level of effort during the expansion amounts to a phone call or a few mouse clicks.

This level of granularity also applies to when you're scaling down. If you spent $200,000 to build a VDI environment for 300 users and you later decide you want to use VDI for only 200 users, well, guess what? You still have a $200,000 VDI environment! But if you're using DaaS, you can just dial back what you're paying for and instantly get the savings. This single-user granularity is great because it makes it quick and efficient to scale up and down. So you have 50 interns coming in for the summer? Tell them to bring their own laptops (whatever they want) and pay a DaaS provider for 50 desktops. When they leave three months later, you stop paying. It's simple and only possible with DaaS.

The costs of DaaS are known

One of the challenges of in-house VDI deployments is that no one really knows what the costs are going to be before the project starts. Sure, you can use some cost calculators and online designers to get an idea, but like any other huge IT project (and VDI is huge!), there's always a string of things you forgot that you'll have to add to the project.

Compare that with DaaS, which has a cost model like this:

[Number of users] × [cost per user] = [cost of DaaS]

Pretty easy! Sure, you've got to consider things like licensing and migration costs and bandwidth and stuff like that, but in terms of the actual costs you're going to incur each month, VDI desktops are a lot more predictable with DaaS as opposed to an in-house VDI project. (We have a chapter about the costs of DaaS later in this book where we'll dig into all the nitty-gritty details.)

DaaS makes for an easy pilot

Since DaaS offers incremental scalability, it makes sense that running a pilot on DaaS is much simpler than setting up an in-house VDI environment for testing. A DaaS pilot is cheap and likely better performing than any old server you have lying around in your lab. You know it works, and you don't have to learn or design anything just to get started. Actually, even if you're thinking about doing in-house VDI, setting up a few users on DaaS is a super-quick and simple way to see if they like the concept of VDI. If they do and it works as you expect it to, you can then figure out whether you should buy more DaaS desktops or start designing and building your own VDI environment.

DaaS providers have better relationships with vendors than you do

One of the very real benefits of DaaS that a lot of people don't talk about is that providers most likely have better relationships with the key hardware and software vendors than you do.

If you use a large DaaS provider that's hosting hundreds of thousands of desktops, you can bet they have a "Bat Phone" connection to Citrix, VMware, Microsoft, Dell, HP, Cisco, and every other vendor they use. Compare that with your own environment, where you have to pay extra for 24/7 support and wait hours just to get your problem escalated to someone who knows what the heck you're talking about. ("Yes, it's plugged in. That's why I'm calling!")

These cozy relationships affect the support DaaS providers are able to get, the costs they pay for their hardware and software, and ultimately the quality of product they're able to offer you.

DaaS extends device lifecycles

One of the advantages of DaaS and VDI is that since your desktops run at full speed in a data center, your users can use any computer—even an older desktop or laptop—and still get decent performance.

The reason we didn't list this back in the section on the advantages of VDI is because if you're building VDI yourself, the cost of the VDI deployment far outweighs the cost savings of reusing an old desktop. In other words, you can't really say "VDI can save me money because I don't have to buy a new $600 desktop PC" if you have to spend $600 per user on your back-end VDI infrastructure!

But when it comes to DaaS, it's a bit more interesting, since DaaS doesn't have the up-front costs. For example, if you're paying $35 per month for DaaS instead of buying a new $600 desktop PC, that's almost two years of DaaS for "free" simply by not buying a new computer. Not bad! (There's a lot more that goes into this calculation, which we'll get into in our chapter on DaaS costs.)

DaaS environments are better than what you can build on your own

The bottom line is that DaaS providers are in the business of providing Windows desktops to customers. That is their product. Your company's product may be laundry soap or financial services or car parts. If you're designing a VDI platform from the IT department of your company, you're just overhead. DaaS providers design VDI environments to be their core product.

In most cases the scale and expertise of a DaaS provider means that they can build and sell you access to a VDI platform that is cheaper, more secure, more reliable, on better hardware, and from more locations than what you can build on your own. Providers have more experts on staff who know more about the VDI platforms, and they have stronger relationships with Citrix, VMware, and Microsoft. In the end, they're just better.

Now this of course doesn't mean that all VDI in the world has to be DaaS, and it doesn't mean that it's foolish to build VDI on your own. You may have security or regulatory requirements that prevent you from moving to DaaS. You may have specific needs and situations that DaaS providers' cookie-cutter approaches can't address. You may want to know your environment is running well and not have to rely on critical support from some low-end engineer on the late shift. Those are all perfectly fine reasons not to move to DaaS. But don't fool yourself into thinking that you can run VDI better than a DaaS provider, because there's a pretty good chance that you can't.

BS Claims from DaaS Providers

Since this is a chapter about the advantages of DaaS, we figured that we should at least mention some of the claims that DaaS providers make in their marketing material that we don't necessarily agree with. We won't go into too much detail on these here, since we cover each of them in other parts of the book, but we want to have a list of them all in one place.

Also, note that several of these BS "advantages" of DaaS are the same BS advantages of VDI we mentioned in the first two chapters. (This makes sense of course, since DaaS is VDI.)

So when you're shopping around for DaaS, here are some of the claims you're going to hear that we don't necessarily agree with:

- **DaaS is cheaper.** Cheaper than what? We agree that DaaS is probably cheaper than building VDI on your own, but it is certainly not cheaper than just buying a $300 desktop for your users. Remember that's okay, though, because DaaS gives you a lot more features than desktop PCs do, so it might be worth the money. It's not cheaper though.

- **DaaS is easier to manage.** Again, easier than what? Sure, DaaS is easier than managing your own VDI environment, since the provider does that for you. But it's not any easier than managing Windows, since you still have to do that with DaaS.

- **DaaS is fully managed.** This is a variation of the "easier management" selling point above. DaaS is fully managed VDI, not fully managed desktops.

- **DaaS is more secure.** As we've mentioned already, it's possible to build a DaaS environment that's more secure than traditional desktop PCs, but it's far from automatic. You don't get better security just because you're moving to DaaS.

- **DaaS provides an optimized user experience.** What does this even mean? Seriously! Several DaaS providers mention it. We guess it means they're using a high-quality remoting protocol like Citrix HDX or Teradici PC-over-IP? That's all well and good, but we would rather just have our desktops running in a nice, fast, thin, light laptop.

So there you have it! A full list of the advantages of DaaS, which we admit look pretty great! Of course it's not all roses, so in our next chapter we're going to look at some of the disadvantages and challenges you'll have to overcome if you want to make DaaS work in your environment.

6. Disadvantages and Challenges of DaaS

Now that we've gone through all the advantages you can get by paying for VDI via DaaS instead of building it yourself, let's take a look at some of the disadvantages and challenges. The good news is that most of the things we'll cover in this chapter have some sort of solution. In fact, that's pretty much what the rest of the book is about. But for now we'll just give you the list so you have it all in one place.

- You have to find a provider to trust.
- The cloud has "unknowns."
- You have to figure out how your desktops will access your files, since they're not in the same place.
- You have to deal with where your desktops run and locality rules.
- You have to determine how you will authenticate your users.

- You might not have any clout in the cloud.
- You're on someone else's repair time.
- The provider might not be flexible in the way you need.
- The provider might not be doing as much as you think.
- DaaS has all the other challenges of VDI we mentioned before.

Let's go over what we mean by each of these.

You have to find a DaaS provider to trust

One of the common threads among projects involving the cloud is trust. Do you trust the DaaS provider? Do you trust their ability to keep your desktops up and running? Do you trust them with your data? Do you trust their security? Do you trust that they won't go out of business?

At the time we're writing this, trust (or lack thereof) is the No. 1 issue we see companies having with cloud providers. Lack of trust stalls more cloud projects than any single technical issue.

The cloud has 'unknowns'

Another big challenge with cloud providers (and one that's closely related to trust) is that, since they are separate companies that make all of their own decisions, providers do a lot of things that you just don't know about. So even if they're the nicest, most trustworthy folks you've ever met, what don't you know about their environment that could come back and bite you? What don't they know even?

We ran into a situation where we were bit by the "unknown" back when we used to run the servers for BrianMadden.com. We had them at a colocation facility where we owned the hardware and networking gear, and the facility provided us with a cage, power, and the network drops. We had two power circuits coming into our cage, and we did all the right things, splitting redundant devices on different circuits, but one day we lost all power anyway.

The reason? It turned out that both of the circuits in our cage were going back to the same PDU in the data center, so when that failed, we lost both circuits. We got burned, as one provider we talked to put it, because we didn't know what we didn't know. Now, of course failures also happen with equipment in your own on-premises data centers, but there's something psychologically different about equipment that you totally own and control versus stuff you outsource. It's something like the peace of mind you get when you *know* you've done everything you can, versus *hoping* your provider has done everything they can.

In addition to trusting your DaaS provider, you also have to sort of trust the DaaS provider's other customers, or trust their ability to isolate customers from each other. For example, what if another customer of your DaaS provider does highly illegal things that cause federal agents to raid the cloud and seize all the equipment for evidence? If your DaaS provider is using a SAN for desktop storage for all of their customers, the police are going to cart the whole thing out and you'll be stuck with no desktops.

Another way you lose control when you outsource your desktops to a DaaS provider is the government can get a court order to monitor or spy on your desktops, and it can order the DaaS provider not to tell you. If you run your own VDI, you'll know if some shifty-eyed types start installing weird USB equipment on your servers, but if you're using DaaS, you might be under total surveillance and have no idea.

Then there's the unknown of connecting your DaaS desktops back to the files, databases, and applications in your onsite data centers. Even if you have secure tunnels, what type of WAN accelerators and caching appliances sit between your site and your cloud desktops? What data is cached on those desktops?

One of the war stories we heard when writing this book was from a client who didn't want any data on the remote desktop, so they had the desktops connect back to files on servers in their office through a VPN. Many of those files were check images, and unfortunately the check image application was written in such a way that it would store the images in the temp folder on the remote desktop. Well, if that application didn't exit properly, it wouldn't clean up those files. Long story short is that one day, one of the employees stumbled upon a temp folder full of check images for hundreds of thousands of dollars! The irony of course is that this company thought they were choosing the secure route by not storing any data in the cloud, but the unknown of how that application worked could have cost them dearly!

One of the unknowns we *don't* worry about, by the way, is rogue employees. We mention this because it's something a lot of people bring up, saying, "I'm nervous that some bad employees might work at the DaaS provider and steal my data." To us, this doesn't make sense for two reasons.

First, a thief who wants to steal data could just as easily work at your company as the DaaS provider. Actually if someone wanted to steal from you, we think it'd be much easier to get a job at the target company, where they could social engineer their way around and go through the trash and stuff. Getting a job at a DaaS provider is probably the worst way to steal from a customer because the provider is going to have all these logs and audits and procedures in place.

Second, you have to remember that a thief is going to be a thief no matter what. Most of today's computer security products are about keeping honest people honest. They're like the locks on the front door of your house. They're really there to make you feel good and to keep the random drunk from stumbling into the wrong house. But if someone really wanted in, they'd just go through a window or pick the door lock. (Seriously, do a YouTube search for that. Door locks slow down actual criminals by about four seconds.)

The point here is that there are unknowns everywhere, and one of the challenges of DaaS is that we can get stuck in a trap of listing out all these far-fetched unknown risks with our DaaS providers even though they have actually been risks for years—it's just that now we're somehow expecting our DaaS providers to meet all these crazy standards that we ourselves have never met.

You have to figure out how your desktops will access your files

As we alluded to in the previous section, another challenge of DaaS is that if you move all your desktops to the cloud, what happens to all the files your users need to access (My Documents, etc.)? Do you move all those files to the cloud provider too? Do you keep them at your location but open a VPN tunnel back? What about other network shares?

And what if you have some users with desktops in your office and others with desktops at the DaaS provider? Do you set up file replication? Do they access their files from the cloud? And what will all these files in the cloud cost? Did you include that in your cost model?

You have to deal with locality rules

One other challenge with DaaS is that even though the whole point of the cloud is that everything is just "out there somewhere," there are a lot of legal and regulatory reasons why you may need to know exactly where your desktops are running and where their disk images and files are stored. For example, do you want your desktops to run from another country? What if that other country has different rules about data security and privacy? Does that expose you legally back in your home country?

What if your desktops are running in another state or locality and you have some legal disagreements with the DaaS provider? Whose laws apply? What if the provider does things with your desktops and your data that are legal in their state but not in yours? Who's responsible for that?

How do you authenticate your users?

If all of your DaaS desktops are in the cloud, how do you authenticate your users? Do you run a domain controller at the provider's data center? Do you expose your LDAP to their site? Do they maintain their own user directory, meaning your users have different usernames and passwords to use their DaaS desktops?

More important, how does the DaaS provider authenticate you (and your users) as humans? In other words, if a user needs to get his password reset, what security questions does he ask? Are they the same security questions that you would ask yourself? Or does the user call you, not your provider?

Remember that your users' jobs are now listed on LinkedIn, and their high school mascot, the street they grew up on, and their favorite TV shows are all on Facebook, so it's probably pretty easy for a criminal to impersonate a user and call the DaaS provider to get his or her account reset. How do you prevent that? (Actually, even when you're administering your users yourself this is something you need to think about.)

Even worse, how do you prevent someone from calling the DaaS provider and impersonating you, the admin? What will the provider do to authenticate you?

You might not have any clout in the cloud

If you work for an enterprise-sized company today, you have buying power. Your company has a relationship with Microsoft, VMware, Citrix, Dell, HP, IBM, Cisco, and whatever other vendors you deal with regularly. No matter whether you buy through partners or direct from the vendors, the odds are that you're not paying list price for anything.

On top of that, if you're in a sector that receives extra discounts (such as education, nonprofit, or government), you're used to getting exceptional prices for the IT products and services you need. So the big question is, "Does that carry over into the DaaS world?"

DaaS providers build their platforms to be efficient, and that efficiency is what makes DaaS a relatively low-cost solution for their customers. Sure, they're making money from the service, so there is a margin, but at the per-desktop level they're not making much. So when it comes to entitled discounts, there's not much room for a price reduction. Does that mean that educational or government institutions can actually assemble their own VDI solutions cheaper than they can outsource them? The answer could quite possibly be yes.

Sure, we argued that you'd be hard-pressed to roll your own VDI solution that's better or cheaper than DaaS, but if there were an opportunity for that to happen, this is it. With steep discounts on hardware and software, the clout you carry on-premises likely outweighs that of cloud, and that's something that you'd have to take into consideration when you decide whether you'll build or buy your VDI.

You're on someone else's repair time

Another challenge (or downside) to DaaS is that when your DaaS isn't working—when things aren't happening as fast as you like—there's not really too much you can do about it.

Imagine if you're desktop environment is down.

Boss: "What's the latest?"
You: "I called them and logged a ticket."
Boss: "What did they say?"
You: "They're working on it."
Boss: (Pauses) "Call them again!"

The irony here is that since the provider is in the sole business of providing DaaS desktops, they are probably (1) better equipped to fix the problem (compared with you), and (2) better motivated to fix the problem (since if it is down too long, they will lose customers and go out of business). None of that helps calm your nerves when there's an outage and there's nothing you can do except wait and trust that your provider is actually working on the problem.

The provider might not be flexible in the ways you need

One of the realities of any cloud service provider is that they make their money by selling cookie-cutter, repeatable solutions. Yeah, their website might claim that their DaaS environment is "100% customizable" (that's a real example!), but really, what the hell does that mean? 100%? Seriously? So you're telling me that I can run Windows 95 desktops with the PC-over-IP protocol at

1600×1200 resolution from a data center in Spain to a file store on Citrix ShareFile in Tasmania?

The point is that when you're building your own VDI environment, you truly do have the option to do whatever you want. You can choose the brand, size, and configuration of the hardware. You choose the storage, the GPU model, the user management tool, the user virtualization product, the hypervisor, the protocol, the systems management tools, and the security solution. The advantage of DaaS is you don't *have* to think about all that stuff. The disadvantage with DaaS is you don't *get* to think about any of that stuff.

Sure, there might be some simple options here and there that you can customize with your DaaS provider, but in general they make money in a high-volume, "rack 'em and stack 'em" kind of way.

And when you do find that DaaS provider that is 100% customizable, you can bet that you're not customizing too much at their $35-per-month entry-level price. Every change you want is going to be like that old Rally's commercial with Seth Green. "Cha-ching!"

The DaaS provider might not be doing as much as you think

We've already talked about how most DaaS providers are only responsible for delivering your desktops to you, and that many of the day-to-day management tasks are still your responsibility. Hopefully you get this by now, but it's still worth mentioning in this section on disadvantages and challenges because some people go into DaaS environments expecting that providers will do a lot more than they actually will.

DaaS has all the other challenges of VDI we mentioned before

Even though this chapter is about the disadvantages and challenges of DaaS environments on top of VDI, remember that DaaS is VDI, so all the disadvantages and challenges of VDI that we mentioned back in Chapter 2 also apply to DaaS. We won't detail them here, but we will list them to jog your memory.

- Users have to have a good internet connection to do any work.
- The Windows desktop user experience is not very good from a tablet or phone.
- Not all applications work via VDI due to graphical and performance limitations.
- Peripherals can be tricky, especially multimedia things like cameras.
- It can be hard to put a price on the benefits you're getting with DaaS (or losing by not going to DaaS).

Now that we're all set with both the advantages and disadvantages of DaaS, let's start stepping through where DaaS makes sense for you.

7. Use Cases for DaaS

So far we've established that DaaS is just VDI that you pay for, we've looked at the advantages and disadvantages of VDI, and we've looked at the advantages and challenges of DaaS. Now let's take a look at the actual reasons people use DaaS.

At this point you might be thinking, "Wait, why is this a chapter? Don't people just use DaaS because they want the benefits of VDI without actually doing the VDI work?" Well, yeah. But it's precisely *because* DaaS is VDI infrastructure with no work that a lot of additional use cases open up where on-premises VDI wouldn't make sense.

At the end of the day, there are as many reasons to use DaaS as there are DaaS customers in the world. But while researching this book, we heard a few use cases again and again that we'd like to call out here, including:

- Customers who have tried VDI, like it, and want to scale up but don't want to deal with the hassle.

- Temporary workers, like contractors or interns.
- Faraway workers, like home office employees or those at remote sites.
- For cloud bursting your VDI.
- For migrating "the rest" of your desktops to your service provider.
- To back up desktops for disaster recovery purposes.
- To convert end-user computing to a known, repeatable cost.
- To avoid being in the infrastructure management business.

Let's take a look at each of these.

Scaling VDI

One of the biggest use cases for DaaS we found was for companies that have tried (and liked) VDI and want to scale up their VDI environments. These companies are great candidates for DaaS because they already know that VDI works for them. They already know how to build their images and what to expect, and now they're just looking for someone else to operate their environment. Plus, with DaaS, they get that incremental scalability we talked about before, which doesn't sound like a big deal until you have to buy a new host, storage, and licenses to expand your environment for just one or two users.

Temporary workers

Building on that, because DaaS allows you to scale up and down on a monthly basis without having to buy more hardware or ending up with extra hardware, it is great for scenarios when you have seasonal or temporary workers or contractors for a project. You can pay for the desktops as your workers need them and then cancel the subscriptions once the workers leave. So all those summer interns who roll into your company with their MacBooks can have a work desktop that doesn't cost you much at all.

Faraway workers

DaaS is also great for faraway workers, like if you have a large office in the U.S. and a few small offices overseas. With DaaS, you can get the benefits of VDI in that you don't have to dictate what actual devices they use, and they can work from the office or home or wherever makes sense in their location.

But then the real DaaS value comes into play because you can choose a DaaS provider that's geographically near to your end users. This means that your users will have a good experience, since they won't have too much latency to their desktops, and you would still get the benefits of VDI and be able to easily manage your users' images and applications.

In fact, you could choose a different DaaS provider for each office, and since you only have to pay for the actual number of desktops you use, you don't have to worry about the overhead and performance of central VDI. And since DaaS means you get VDI without the complexity of having to build it, you could do this for *very* small environments. If you're a company in California with 500 employees and you want to send two people to Australia to work there, just find some Australian DaaS provider to host their two desktops for your line-of-business apps, and let the two mates you're sending over there choose whatever laptops they want to use.

Cloud bursting your on-premises VDI

Another potential use case for DaaS is something called cloud bursting (also called hybrid cloud). The idea here is that you combine traditional on-premises VDI with public cloud-based VDI (DaaS). Ideally, you hook them together with the same front-end or the same framework so you can use your on-premises environment for most of your users but then "burst" to the cloud if you run out of capacity in your own VDI environment.

This is nice because it lets you build a smaller VDI environment in-house for your day-to-day needs, but then if there's a snowstorm or something and you have a lot more demand for VDI than most days, your users can still get in and you pay only for what you actually use.

The downside to cloud bursting or hybrid cloud DaaS is that at the time of this writing, the providers' vision about how awesome this is may be a few steps ahead of what's actually possible. For example, VMware's on-premises VDI solution is Horizon View, and their DaaS solution, while called Horizon DaaS, is Desktone's DaaS platform, which they recently bought. Right now the two do not integrate at all, so you run one platform in-house and the DaaS provider runs another. Yeah, VMware's vision is awesome, and eventually they'll make it so you can seamlessly pull together desktop sessions from either location, but as of today, that's a bullet point on a roadmap slide, not an actual feature. (We don't mean to pick on VMware here, by the way—Citrix is in the same boat.)

That doesn't mean that no one's tried it though. We spoke to some cloud providers who are hosting the on-premises versions of the VDI software in their cloud (XenDesktop, Horizon View, etc.) to allow their customers to bridge their on-premises VDI environments with the cloud provider's. We thought this was pretty exciting, but it turns out this might not be so popular.

Think about it. Why do people build their own in-house VDI environments instead of using DaaS? Typically because they have regulatory, security, or trust issues around the cloud, or they need more flexibility than what a provider will offer or just flat out think they can do it better. (Or they just prefer to do things on-premises.) Fine.

And why do people choose to rent their VDI from DaaS providers? Because they don't want to deal with the complexity of designing and building their own VDI and they believe the DaaS providers can do it better and cheaper.

What's interesting is that those two sets of reasons are mutually exclusive! A company that decides to build their own VDI does so for reasons that cause them not to want to use DaaS, and a company that decides on DaaS does so for the specific reason that they don't want to deal with building their own VDI.

So the *actual* use case of the hybrid cloud almost turns out to be a migration path from on-premises VDI to cloud-hosted DaaS:

1. You start with VDI.
2. You want to grow or burst your VDI to the cloud.
3. You do that once.
4. You think, "Wow, that was awesome. Why am I dealing with my own VDI at all?"

Hello DaaS migration!

Migrating 'the rest' of your infrastructure to your service provider

We're getting to the point—especially in the small and midsize business world—where companies are moving most, if not all, of their server infrastructure to cloud providers. In those cases, moving their Windows desktops to the cloud makes sense. They get their desktops to run right next to their data and applications. Plus, many of these companies weren't that great at running their desktops to begin with, often replacing things when they broke instead of on a regular basis. In these situations, tying up the loose ends is an excellent use case for DaaS. Everything's moving to the cloud, so let's do that with our desktops too!

Disaster recovery purposes

Another use case for DaaS is for disaster recovery. In this context, we're talking about a situation where you already have VDI and you're looking for a solution in case something happens at your data center that takes those desktops offline. (So think of this use case as backup for your VDI rather than backup VDI for your traditional desktops.)

A lot of companies have disaster recovery solutions in place for traditional desktops, but these typically involve large spaces full of old computers one notch down on the PC replacement cycle, not to mention another server room full of duplicated servers. These parallel environments are a huge waste of time and money for space and maintenance just to have something in your back pocket for a rainy day.

The concept, at least in our dreams, is to build a VDI environment that is so sleek, so well run, and so manageable that in the event of a significant outage you could take the desktop images to a DaaS provider and spin them up in a very short period of time.

Of course from a practical standpoint, there's a lot more to it, since you have to:

- Make sure you provision the right desktops to the right users.
- Get the users access to the data they need to do their jobs.
- Get the users access to the desktops.
- Deal with a virtually infinite number of little things that could go wrong in a situation like this.

Still, it's not impossible, especially if you can find a way to dial back the desktop images to a bare-minimum set of applications that employees need to do their jobs (after all, this is a disaster scenario we're talking about) and you've managed to plan to have backups of your data and application servers at the provider as well.

Actually, companies that fall under this use case are probably better candidates for IaaS (Infrastructure as a Service) across the board, keeping all of their services duplicated in the cloud. (People are calling this DRaaS for Disaster Recovery as a Service. Seriously.) Doing so would also solve the problem of getting the data, provisioning, and access figured out, since everything would all be there to begin with.

Another caution here (which we'll discuss more later) is that you need to make sure that your DaaS provider actually has the capacity to fulfill all of their commitments if a large-scale disaster happens. If you and all your neighboring companies have all chosen the same DaaS provider and something happens in your city, how do you know that your DaaS provider won't be overloaded and unable to fulfill everything? Even if they have enough hardware, do they have the staff, the internet connections, and the processes in place for a near-instant 10-times workload increase?

The final argument to be made here is that if you've gone through all this effort to replicate every aspect of your business in a cloud provider, why aren't you just using DaaS and IaaS in the first place? Maybe this is the impetus to make that happen!

Converting end-user computing to a known, repeatable cost

The traditional desktop lifecycle is a series of unpredictable peaks and valleys. You buy a laptop, which is a huge one-time expense, then you try to make it last as long as you can. You have to pay to fix it here and there. You have to replace old, lost, broken, and stolen ones.

If you build VDI, you can get out of some of these cost spikes, but now you have to pay for the VDI servers and buy storage and licenses and deal with all that. Plus, scaling out results in more cost spikes.

DaaS can be the best of both worlds. With DaaS, your costs are fixed operational expenditures instead of jarring capital expenditures. Sure, you're going to pay those costs forever, but at least you know exactly what those costs are. And, frankly, that's how a lot of business expenses are moving anyway (for example, cloud Software as a Service versus on-premises, mobile phones subsidized by carriers based on service, or subscribing to Spotify instead of buying individual tracks). This is the direction that everything is moving in anyway, so why not get your end-user computing on board too?

Avoiding the infrastructure management business

Everyone knows that the actual reason you run Windows on all your desktops is that you have Windows applications. Since those apps are starting to move to web-based offerings (internal or cloud), it's tempting to think that your life is going to get easier now that you have "less Windows." Unfortunately, it only takes one long-tail critical Windows app to ruin that whole vision. After all, your last Windows app still requires a Windows operating system, which means you have to deal with all the patching, management, and maintenance that Windows requires.

In the old days (or the current days), when you had a whole slew of Windows applications, justifying the enormous amount of time you spent managing the entire monolithic stack, including the hardware, OS, applications, profiles, and data, was easy. But as the number of Windows applications starts to decrease, the amount of work you have to do to manage the desktops stays pretty much the same.

At some point, you're going to realize that the level of effort you put into managing Windows desktops will be too great compared with the actual benefit you get from having the Windows apps, and you'll have to make a decision about how you want to spend your time. For that situation, DaaS can be the solution. You get to have the Windows apps without having to manage Windows on all your clients, and the copy of Windows that runs in the DaaS environment can be much less hassle to maintain than in the days when everything was physical.

One of the people we interviewed for this book (an end-user customer of DaaS) summed up this idea by saying, "Look, we can all agree that Windows as a desktop platform is going away. Maybe not this year. Maybe not next year. But it's declining. So at what point do I say, 'Why am I continuing to invest all these resources in a dying platform?' Instead, we're going to package up the Windows apps we have to have, ship them to the cloud, and spend our time doing more strategic things."

8. Licensing :(

Now that we've gotten through all the advantages and disadvantages and the "Should you or shouldn't you?" part of the book, we can finally get into the dirty details of making DaaS work. The next few chapters are about some of the lower-level design decisions you need to make when you decide you want to move to DaaS.

Let's start with licensing for DaaS environments. We've broken this up into s discussion about the Windows OS licenses you need and then a look at how applications are licensed.

Understanding Windows Licensing in DaaS Environments

There are two things we'll open the conversation with around Microsoft Windows licensing in DaaS environments.

First, all this talk about saving money with DaaS—if that's even possible—does not come from licensing savings. You still need all the same licenses in a DaaS environment as you do in a traditional one. (Actually, sometimes you need more for DaaS.)

Second, since this entire book is about desktops from the cloud that run Windows, you are at the mercy of Microsoft. Windows and Office are Microsoft products, and they get to make the rules. Unfortunately, their rules suck. Thousands of articles have been written about how Microsoft is stuck in the past and struggling to transform from a company that sells software in boxes for desktops to the new web-based mobile world where people aren't anchored to their desks. Clearly, Microsoft is struggling.

While we have lots of ideas about what Microsoft should do (or what they *need* to do) around modernizing Windows licensing, that's a topic for another book. The wretched reality is that when you're talking about moving Microsoft Windows desktops into the cloud via DaaS, you have to play by Microsoft's rules. If you don't like them, your options are to (1) not use DaaS, or (2) not use Windows. (And if the latter were so easy, you would have migrated away by now. Ah, the joys of a monopoly!)

Windows desktop licenses

The first thing to know about Windows licensing is the importance of the word "license." You do not *buy* the Windows software. You buy a *license* for the Windows software that grants you certain rights. So right off the bat you have to understand that when you buy the license, you agree to its stupid rules. The whole internet troll objection of "What? Why are they telling me what I can do with MY software?" is a farce. It isn't your software. It's Microsoft's. They're just selling you some rights to do certain things with it.

Microsoft desktop products like Windows 7, Windows 8, and Windows 8.1 (which are actually called Windows client operating systems in Microsoft license-speak) have several licensing options.

If you walk into a consumer retail store and buy a laptop with Windows 8 preinstalled on it, part of what you pay for is a license that allows you to run Windows 8 on that laptop. What a lot of people don't know is that license is for the right to run Windows

8 on that laptop only. You're not allowed to take that copy of Windows 8 and install it on another laptop. Even if you remove it from the original laptop, you're not allowed to run it anywhere else.

Obviously that's a bummer and a huge limitation to that type of license. (That type of license, by the way, is called an OEM license because the OEM that makes the laptop buys the license from Microsoft, and then that license is transferred, along with the cost, to you when you buy the laptop.)

The next type of Windows client OS license is the Full Packaged Product (FPP) license, which is what you get if you walk into a store and buy a standalone copy of the Windows software or if you buy a downloadable version of Windows from Microsoft.com. A lot of people commonly refer to these FPP licenses as retail licenses, and you can get them in both standalone and upgrade versions.

Just like when you buy a new laptop with Windows preinstalled, when you buy the Windows FPP software you are entering into a legal agreement with Microsoft where you agree to use the software only in the ways they outline. The exact rights you have vary depending on what you buy and what country you're in, but Microsoft generally controls things like how many devices you're allowed to install the software on, whether (or how often) you're allowed to transfer the software to a different device after you initially installed it, and even whether you're allowed to use the software for commercial purposes. (So yeah, probably 99% of home-based businesses are in violation of Microsoft license agreements. Fun.)

The third type of Microsoft Windows client license is the Volume License, or VL. This is for customers who are buying more than one license (hence the "volume" part). In other words, you could think of the VL as the business or commercial license for Windows. There are actually several different VL programs tuned for different size customers, with all sorts of marketing-friendly names, such as Open Value, Select Plus, and Enterprise Agreement. Each of these programs gives the buyer (err, licensee) different rights to do varying things with Windows for some amount of time. These are known as Product Usage Rights, or PURs, in Microsoft-speak.

For example, some VL programs allow you to use the software forever, while others are subscription-based and you have to stop using it once you stop paying. Some programs let your users use the products from their home computers, while others allow use from company-owned computers only. Some VL programs make you pay for copies of Windows for every computer you have, while others base it on the number of employees you have. It's not worth going through the details of each program here, since they vary by country and they change all the time. The important thing is that since VDI and DaaS are for businesses, you'll be buying some type of VL, and you'll need to ensure that the specific VL you end up with has PURs that allow you to have your Windows desktops running on someone else's (the DaaS provider's) hardware. (Quick side note: Do you ever read sentences like that, with stupid acronyms like VL and PUR, in a chapter of a book about the intricacies of Microsoft licensing and sigh, thinking, "What the hell happened to my life? I just wanted to get a job with computers, and after all these years, *this* is what I do now?" It could be worse though. At least you're not writing a book about it!)

Licensing Windows clients as a service

Let's tie this conversation back to DaaS. With DaaS, you're paying to use a Microsoft Windows desktop running in someone else's data center, so obviously that Windows desktop has to be properly licensed. In the case of DaaS, you typically pay a monthly fee for each desktop you want to access, and you stop paying when you no longer need to access that desktop.

To license the desktop, most people assume that either (1) the DaaS provider has "pre-bought" enough Windows client licenses to cover their customers, or (2) the DaaS provider pays Microsoft a few dollars each month for each user to cover the cost of them using Windows. Both of those options seem straightforward enough, which is unfortunate, because neither of them is real.

The first option (where the provider pre-buys a bunch of licenses for its customers) doesn't work because the various Microsoft license agreements (the PURs of the VL) are for companies that will use the licenses internally. In other words, a hosting provider can't buy a Windows license and then let non-internal employees (i.e., your DaaS users) use those licenses.

The second option doesn't work either. While it's true that Microsoft has a licensing program called the Service Provider License Agreement (SPLA) that's designed for this exact use case (hosting providers who want to offer software services to external customers), Microsoft specifically *excludes* Windows client licenses from the SPLA program.

WTF? WTF? WTF? WTF? WTF? WTF? WTF? WTF? WTF? WTF?

(Seriously, that is messed up!)

Why would Microsoft create a SPLA program and then not allow it to be used with the licenses for Windows 7 and Windows 8? Or another way to phrase that question is, "Why is Microsoft making it hard to do DaaS?" After all, if Microsoft allowed Windows client licenses to be covered by SPLA, it would be simple for customers to move off of Windows on their laptops and instead they could . . . Oh. Perhaps we just answered our own question.

This is the single most messed-up, backwards, mean-spirited, asinine thing you're going to read about in this entire book. In fact, one of us (Brian) actually quit the Microsoft MVP program in protest. (His actions changed nothing.)

Given these crazy restrictions from Microsoft, how is it possible for Windows-based DaaS to even exist? How does anyone use DaaS legally? There are a few options:

- Use the Windows Server OS as your "desktop."
- Buy your own regular Windows desktop licenses to cover your DaaS desktops.
- Switch to Linux.

Let's look at the pros and cons of each of these.

Use Windows Server as your 'desktop' OS

We said that the Microsoft SPLA program is the perfect licensing vehicle for Windows desktop licenses in DaaS environments, but that Microsoft does not include the Windows client OSes in the SPLA program.

Microsoft *does* include remote access to Windows *Server* OSes in the SPLA program, via a per-month Remote Desktop Services Client Access License, or RDS CAL. So if your DaaS hoster builds you a DaaS environment based on Windows Server instead of Windows 7, they can build in the cost of the Windows license rental and you only have to pay for what you actually use for as long as you use it.

This actually isn't *that* bad, and it's what most providers do. Note that this doesn't necessarily mean that you're accessing a terminal services/RDSH shared-session desktop. Most DaaS providers still build an environment that is just like VDI, where each user has his own dedicated virtual machine running Windows. The only difference is that this is a Server OS instead of a client OS.

It's even possible to disguise the server OS so it looks like a client. You can install something called the "Desktop Experience" feature, which makes Windows Server 2012 look just like Windows 8 (or Windows Server 2008 R2 look just like Windows 7), with the only real difference being the product name and license under the hood. The fact that you can dress up a Windows Server to look like a client prompts many people—ourselves included—to ask Microsoft why they allow such a loophole instead of just offering a SPLA license for Windows clients, but unfortunately we learned that logic and practicality do not apply when speaking with Microsoft about licensing. (We also want to be careful about what we wish for, because if we make too much noise, Microsoft might just disable the features that allow Windows Server to look like a desktop and then we'd all be screwed.)

Buy your own Windows desktop licenses for your DaaS environment

If you really want to have a "regular" Windows desktop OS in your DaaS environment, the only way that's possible is to buy the licenses from Microsoft and then let your DaaS provider know that you have your own licenses. This scenario is called BYOL, or bring your own licenses.

Unfortunately (as expected) this isn't as straightforward as you might hope. First of all, since you're a business, you have to buy your licenses through one of the VL programs. The FPP licenses and the OEM licenses do not include the right to run your Windows desktops on servers in someone else's data center. Actually, many of the VL programs do not allow that option either. If you want to run your Windows desktops on someone else's hardware, that right is granted to you via a Microsoft license called Virtual Desktop Access, or VDA. So you need a VDA for every desktop you want to run in your DaaS provider's cloud.

How you get a VDA license depends on the device you're buying it for. If the device is capable of running Windows locally (like if it's a desktop PC or laptop), you cannot simply buy VDA for it. Instead, you have to have (or buy) a Windows client OS license and then buy Software Assurance (SA) for that device (which you pay for year by year) and your SA subscription includes VDA. If you're using a device like a thin client or iPad, which cannot run Windows locally, then you *can* buy VDA directly for it. (The MSRP for VDA is $100 per year, per device, though your locality or reseller might offer it for a different price.)

If that sounds confusing and messed up, it's because it is, for several reasons.

First, if you're accessing your Windows DaaS desktop from a PC or laptop, you have to pay for (or have paid in the past for) a full Windows client license, and then on top of that you have to pay annually for SA. So with the whole idea that DaaS can be cheaper because you can "reuse your old desktop," just remember that you're paying for SA this whole time.

The second shitty thing is that SA and VDA apply to *devices*, not users, and you have to buy them for every company-owned device that users use to access their remote Windows desktop.

What's crazy about this is this only applies to *company-owned* devices. It does not apply to users' personal devices. So if you buy your users iPads as additional devices they can use to access their DaaS desktops, you have to buy VDA for them for an additional $100 per iPad per year. Are you buying corporate mobile phones for your users? There's another $100, per phone, per year. Again, this only applies to company-owned devices, because you can't know what or how many devices a user uses when he or she is outside the office. So Microsoft basically says, "As long as you make sure you have VDA on all the devices the company owns, we'll let it slide when users connect from their own devices."

Now here's where it gets *really* crazy. If a user brings a personal, non-company-owned device into the office, you also have to buy a VDA license for it in order for it to access a remote VDI or DaaS desktop! And remember, VDA licenses are purchased for devices, not for users, so if you have a device-loving user who brings in various devices over the course of the year, you need to buy a $100-per-year VDA subscription *for each of them!*

How in the heck are you supposed to police and track that? Seriously, we have no idea. Maybe you put a metal detector at the entrance to your building and x-ray everyone's bags so you can track which devices they use? It's insane. (And we've actually left a lot of details out here for the sake of simplicity. There are all sorts of rules about primary devices and how personal devices need to be licensed differently if the user doesn't have a device at the workplace, not to mention language around how the "workplace" is defined and this whole concept of Companion Device Licenses. Seriously. It's insane.)

But wait. There's more! Let's say that you're actually following this and you're on board so far. You want to use DaaS for your desktops, and you've decided that you'll pay for the necessary SA and VDA licenses for all the company-owned client devices as well as personal devices that users bring into the office. Great. So now you want to go to your DaaS provider with your own VDA licenses.

If you want to use your own VDA licenses for DaaS (which you have to do, since the DaaS provider can't buy them for you), your DaaS provider must have isolated hardware instances for anything that runs Microsoft software for each of their customers! So you know that awesome virtualization thing that allows multiple VMs to run on the same physical hardware? Yeah, your DaaS providers can't do that with VDA. They have to build separate physical hardware for each of their customers. That means if you only want to host a few users for DaaS on Windows 7, it's probably going to cost you a fortune because the provider is going to have to buy hardware they will have to dedicate to you. Again, this goes against the whole point of the efficiencies of virtualization. What is the point of this? What is Microsoft gaining besides making it hard for people to . . . Oh, whoops. We just answered our own question again!

Switch to Linux

Okay, so we admit that we added the "switch to Linux" option as a sort of joke, but after reading all this crap about Microsoft licensing, you may be seriously considering it. (Or, more realistically, your boss might look at your Microsoft licensing invoice and ask whether it's possible to switch to Linux.)

So here's the deal. One of the main uses for DaaS today is specifically as a way to handle all those Windows apps that users want to access from wherever they happen to be. In other words, you pretty much have to use Windows because your enterprise apps are Windows. If you didn't have Windows apps, well, you probably wouldn't replace them with Linux apps. You'd probably replace them with HTML5 or web or SaaS apps so you wouldn't have to be dealing with this old-style desktop computing model.

That said, you have Windows apps for a reason, switching would be a mess, and Microsoft knows it. Monopoly on!

What license option should you pick? SPLA or VDA?

To recap, in order to use a "real" client OS (like Windows 7) with DaaS, you have to buy the VDA license yourself, and your provider can't run any of your Windows desktop environment on the same hardware as any other customer. These two stipulations mean that the only customers who are getting Windows client-based DaaS are medium and large businesses who have long-term commitments to DaaS (since they have to buy the VDA licenses up front) and have enough users to make it worthwhile for the provider to dedicate hardware to the business.

The rest of the world—small businesses, companies with seasonal workers, and people who want to try DaaS, among others—have to buy DaaS from a provider who is able to bundle in the Microsoft Windows license via the SPLA program. The SPLA program *does* allow providers to share their hardware with multiple customers (which is how it should be), but again, remember that SPLA applies only to the Windows Server OSes. So if you're using SPLA, you're getting Windows Server dressed up to look like a desktop. (The other advantage of SPLA over VDA is that SPLA is licensed per user, so you don't have to frisk your users as they walk in the door in search of additional non-company-owned devices you'd have to license.)

So really that's what it comes down to. If you're big and committed to DaaS, you can have your choice of VDA (for Windows 7 or 8) or you can just pay your DaaS provider for everything and get Windows Server desktops via SPLA. If you're small or just testing out DaaS, you don't have a choice—you're getting a server desktop. This is how all the consumer DaaS providers do it. When you sign up for that Amazon Web Services WorkSpaces desktop, you're getting a Windows Server 2008 R2 desktop.

Microsoft Office Licensing for DaaS

Can you believe that all that licensing talk over the last several pages was just about the Windows OS itself? We haven't even started talking about how you license the applications that run in your desktop yet!

While we'd love to have a single section on just application licensing, one of the main—if not *the* main—applications people like to use in their DaaS environments is Microsoft Office. Unfortunately Microsoft Office is made by Microsoft, the creator of the FPP, PUR, SA, VDA, and SPLA shenanigans we just reviewed. So do you think Microsoft Office licensing is simple and straightforward? Of course not!

Alas, we have to cover Microsoft Office licensing in DaaS environments as a separate topic. Then we'll move on to the normal ways that every other non-Microsoft application in the world is licensed.

Office licensing basics

Microsoft Office licensing shares many common traits with Microsoft Windows OS licensing. Like Windows, the Microsoft Office Suite comes in several versions (Office 2010, Office 2013, Office 365) and editions (Professional, Standard, etc.). Also like the Windows OS licenses, you don't actually buy the Microsoft Office software. Rather, you buy a license that grants you rights to do certain things with that software while prohibiting other things.

Also like the Windows OS, there are various licensing programs for Office, including SPLA (that Service Provider License Agreement), geared toward companies that host Office, like DaaS providers. There are also various VL programs for companies, including the yearly SA subscriptions, which confer additional rights.

Office Volume Licensing

Most companies that use Office buy their licenses through one of the VL programs. Office bought in this way is licensed *per device*. If a company also pays for SA for Office, they get additional benefits, such as roaming and remote usage rights. Roaming usage rights allow the primary user of a licensed device to also use Office on additional devices, and remote rights allow users to access remote copies of Office, like in DaaS scenarios.

So at first you think, "Okay, cool, so as long as I buy SA I can bring my own Office licenses to my DaaS provider, meaning I don't have to pay more."

The answer, of course, depends. The remote usage rights included with SA for Office only allow users to remotely access Office running on hardware that you own or that is dedicated to you. So it's the same thing as the VDA versus SPLA rights from Windows. If you are accessing Windows 7 or Windows 8 desktops via your own VDA licenses from a DaaS provider that's hosting your DaaS environment on hardware that's dedicated to you, then yes, you can use your existing Office licenses (with SA) to access that environment.

But if you're accessing a shared hosted environment, you will have to buy additional Office licenses.

Office SPLA licensing

If you'd like pay-as-you-go Office licenses for your DaaS desktops, you can do that by paying a per-month, per-user fee to your DaaS provider (which your DaaS provider forwards back to Microsoft). In these cases, Office is licensed per user rather than per client device. The copy of Office you use is the full normal version, but you only get the rights to use it on the DaaS provider's remote desktop. In other words, if you also want to run Office on some local computers, you'd have to buy Office separately for them.

The catch is that your DaaS provider is only allowed to provide SPLA-based access to Office from DaaS environments running on server OSes. So if you're running Windows 7 or Windows 8 in your DaaS, you have to bring your own Office licenses (which stinks, but since that's what you're doing for your Windows licenses, it's to be expected).

Licensing Other Applications

Now that we've dealt with Microsoft licensing, the last thing we have to look at is application licenses—all the Windows desktop applications that you're actually running in your DaaS desktops. Fortunately this is simple compared with what you have to go through with Microsoft!

Obviously there are millions of applications in the world from thousands of different software companies, so we can't cover all the various intricacies of every situation. (But again, seriously, compared with Microsoft licensing everything else is simple.)

Let's start by listing some questions you should ask your application maker about how their licensing works.

- Is the application licensed per user or per device?
- If it's per user, is it per named user or per concurrent user?
- If it's per named user, how often are you allowed to switch the named users? (Once every 90 days, once a month, etc.?)

- If it's per device, does it matter who owns the device? (The company or the user?)
- If it's per device, does it matter where the user is when he or she uses the application? (In the company's office versus outside in the world?)
- Are there any restrictions around running the application in a remote Windows desktop?
- Does it matter if the application is run on hardware that is owned by a DaaS provider?
- Is it okay to run the application on a server OS instead of a desktop OS?

It's not uncommon to find application makers who don't have the answer to all of these questions. (Heck, it's not uncommon to find yourself explaining what VDI or DaaS is.) Actually, for application makers who don't really know the answers, we just sort of don't tell them what we're doing and try to make the decisions that feel right. As long as you're buying the same number of licenses you'd use in your non-DaaS physical environment, you should be fine. We call this the "straight-face test." If you can explain how your licensing plan is legitimate to the vendor while keeping your face straight and not busting out in awkward laughter, you can probably feel good about how you've licensed an application.

One final thing about application licensing that we'll mention here is that we're big fans of using software asset management tools to track which users use each application (and how often), and then adjusting your purchasing or renewals of licenses based on actual use. This is one of the things that could have been technically difficult in a distributed laptop-based world, but in DaaS environments, where everyone is on centralized servers, it's much easier. Seriously, look into this when you go to DaaS. You could be wasting huge amounts of money on licenses for people who never use specific applications.

Once you recognize that there are certain users who don't use certain apps, there are ways to manage users' access to those applications, but we'll get to that when we talk about image management a bit later on.

9. The Cost of DaaS

It seems like many of the people selling DaaS claim that it is "cheaper" than traditional desktops, and many people moving to DaaS do so because the "costs are known." Since cost is such a big part of the DaaS conversation, studying and understanding the true cost of DaaS is an important part of figuring out how to use DaaS in your own environment.

Buying Versus Renting

One of the most important things that we'll open with is that with DaaS—especially compared with VDI—you transfer much of your cost from capex to opex. (We discussed capex versus opex back in Chapter 5.) One of the realities of this arrangement is that it's possible that your opex can be higher with DaaS, but with little to no capex. So is that good or bad? Really it depends on what's important to you as a company.

Another important reality with DaaS is that you're essentially just renting your desktops instead of buying them. The same is true for the Microsoft Windows and Office SPLA licenses we discussed in the previous chapter. Once you stop paying for your DaaS, you lose access to your environment.

This is one of the things that commenters to our blog mention again and again as a disadvantage of DaaS. "If I ever stop paying my DaaS bill," they argue, "then I have nothing to show for it." They compare that with on-premises VDI with perpetual application licenses, because in those cases, they argue, "at least I have something when I'm done."

Okay, we get their point, but we still don't agree. If you buy your servers and you buy your licenses, after three years what do you have? Three-year-old servers and three-year-old products. And yeah, you didn't have to pay anything for them for the past three years, but you sure spent a pile of money up front for them—money that could have been used for other things if you didn't blow it all at the start. And now that everything is old, you have to buy new servers and new software and start the cycle all over again.

The thing to keep in mind is that yes, having a commitment to a provider "forever" might seem like it's more expensive in the long run, but if you honestly look at the spikey nature of buying new hardware and software every few years, we're not so sure. And we have a cost model to prove it!

A Note About Cost Models

We already noted back in Chapter 2 that our VDI book includes an entire chapter about how cost models are total BS. (So never mind about that cost model we just mentioned in the first section.) Again, if you're curious about why cost models are BS, you can google [how to lie with cost models] to find our article, but here's the gist.

First, with cost models—especially those that compare two different ways of doing things—it's easy to include or exclude elements that make the model turn out your way.

THE COST OF DAAS • 93

Second, cost models are totally worthless when trying to compare things that are too different. So if you want to do a cost analysis of traditional desktop computing versus VDI (or, God forbid, traditional desktops versus DaaS), forget it. You can't do it. There are just too many assumptions and unknowns, and any comparison you make will be worthless.

Now, if you want to compare the costs of VDI versus the costs of DaaS, okay, now that's possible, since those are pretty close to each other.

Third, the downfall of cost models is soft costs. Sure, soft costs are real, but quantifying them in a model is not possible. People say all kinds of crap, like, "The old system took 60 seconds to boot up, and the new system only takes 30 seconds, so that's 30 seconds per day saved, 2.5 minutes per week, 130 minutes per year. If we have 500 employees and the average cost is $40 per hour, then shaving 30 seconds from our boot-up time saves the company $43k per year!"

No, it doesn't.

We could go on, but you get the point we're making. That said, technology does cost money. Traditional desktops cost money, VDI desktops cost money, and DaaS desktops cost money. Understanding that every environment is different, we can *very broadly* rank these three desktop options, in order of cost, as:

1. On-premises VDI (most expensive)
2. DaaS
3. Traditional desktop PCs (least expensive)

Again, as we've said, the fact that VDI and DaaS are more expensive than traditional desktop PCs is okay. You're getting so many more features for your money, so it's worth it as long as you can deal with the limitations. As for DaaS, it also makes sense that a DaaS provider can do it cheaper than you can, since they have economies of scale and dedicated expertise.

Digging into DaaS Costs

Let's take a look at what really goes into the total dollar cost of a DaaS environment. The good news is that all the DaaS providers we spoke with were forthcoming and honest about their pricing. (They don't all post pricing on their websites, but we feel that's more because they have so many options as opposed to them being shady about pricing.) The bad news is that the literal price of a DaaS desktop represents only a fraction of the total cost of their DaaS environment. Other factors that affect the total cost of your DaaS environment include:

- Management costs
- Additional server costs
- Costs for things "left behind" in your customer environment
- DaaS platform options
- Persistent versus non-persistent disk images
- Type of user licensing (named user versus concurrent)
- Overcommitment
- Microsoft licensing models
- Migration costs (to move to DaaS in the first place)

Let's examine each of these.

Management costs

Underscoring what we've said already, the single most important thing to understand when calculating the cost of your DaaS environment is that the price you get per desktop from your DaaS provider isn't anywhere close to the amount of money you'll actually need to spend each month to put your desktops in the cloud. It might not even be the amount of money you give the DaaS provider by the end of the project!

The reason for this, as we've discussed already, is that the DaaS provider only does so much. (Or, put another way, even when you move to DaaS, there are lot of leftover things that you still have to do.) Here's a partial list of the tasks you might have to do or the things you might have to deal with after moving to DaaS:

- Installing, configuring, maintaining, and managing Windows applications
- Printing
- Dealing with files and data location
- Data access
- Network access
- Internet access
- Internal applications
- Updates
- Backups
- User account maintenance
- Image management
- Endpoint device management
- Remote support
- Mobile device support

In most cases, moving to DaaS removes none of these responsibilities from your list. So while you might be able to reduce head count or avoid hiring a few folks with the qualifications necessary to deploy a complex storage or VDI solution, the tasks that your desktop support staff do are largely unchanged.

Additional server costs

One of the things we'll get to in the next few chapters is a conversation about the location and design of your supporting servers. Yeah, it's great that DaaS moves your desktops into the cloud, but now what about your email servers, file servers, databases, application servers, and so on?

If you also choose to move those to the cloud, or if your desktop environment *requires* that you move some of them to the cloud, you'll also need to calculate the costs of hosting, managing, and maintaining those.

What's left in your on-premises location?

We've already mentioned that DaaS doesn't remove *all* technology from your on-premises location. Your users will still need desktop PCs, laptops, or thin clients to access their remote DaaS desktops. How much do those cost? Who fixes them when they break? How long will they last?

You also have to deal with the network, especially in medium-to-large-size office locations. We imagine you didn't think too much about the speed of your internet connection before you moved to DaaS, but now that you have fifty users who each want 300 Kbps (or whatever it is for you) for a decent desktop connection, you're looking at a pretty substantial network upgrade when you flip the switch to DaaS.

And what about all your other physical IT assets in your office? Even after DaaS you'll need someone to make sure the printers are online. You need someone to manage your WiFi access points and your internet connection. None of that goes away when you move to DaaS.

DaaS platform differences

We talked a bit about the various Windows platform options for DaaS. Providers can fit more user sessions on Terminal Server (now called Remote Desktop Session Host, or RDSH) session-based desktops as opposed to giving each user his or her own virtual machine. So if your desktop environment is basic enough that RDSH will work instead of VMs, you can save a significant chunk of money by getting your DaaS provider to provide RDSH session-based desktops to your users.

DaaS image types

We'll dig more into disk images in the next chapter, but from what we've seen so far, some DaaS providers offer non-persistent shared disk images more cheaply than fully persistent images. So the type of image you want can affect the price you pay per desktop.

Total users versus concurrent users

Some DaaS providers give you the ability to pay for the number of concurrent users separately from the number of named users. Named users would be the total number of different users set up in the DaaS platform, while concurrent users is how many are logged on at the same time.

For most DaaS providers, no distinction is made between these types of users. You pay them for the number of user desktops you'd like to use, and then you pay the same amount each month regardless of whether they're all logged in at once or you have only a handful logged in at a time.

But some DaaS providers will let you specify the number of total users versus concurrent users. So, for example, you could pay for 1,000 unique user accounts but only for 500 simultaneously active users. What this means, in effect, is that you are paying the DaaS provider for the cold storage for 1,000 different users, but they only provide to you the VDI hosting infrastructure to support 500 sessions. If you can work this out, it's much cheaper than paying for 1,000 users who could all run at once. But then again, if you only pay for 500 concurrent users and you actually get 500 users logged on at the same time, user number 501 would get an error saying the system is full.

Microsoft licenses

As we outlined (in painstaking detail) in the last chapter, the type of Microsoft license you have will also affect the cost of your DaaS environment. If you want to use a Windows desktop OS (Windows 7 or 8, for example) for your DaaS environment, you have to buy your own Windows client licenses (a capital expenditure) and then pay for SA each year. In most cases when a DaaS provider quotes a price to host Windows 7 desktops for you, they're not including the cost of SA or VDA in that price. So you have to be aware that that's something you're going to be paying for in addition to the DaaS costs.

On the other hand, if your DaaS provider is using Windows Server instances as their desktops, then their environment can be covered by SPLA, which means you don't have any up-front costs and you can cancel anytime. (Obviously this is a better choice for DaaS, but if you need Windows 7, it's not a choice for you.)

Don't Forget About the Cost of the Migration

The final thing we'd like to mention as we talk about the costs of DaaS is the cost of the migration to DaaS. If you thought signing up for the DaaS provider was the end of the road, you'd be wrong. After all, you have to somehow get all the desktops and applications from your company into the DaaS provider's cloud. This is no small task. It's an all-out forklift of a desktop migration, and you're in the driver's seat!

There will almost certainly be costs associated with this, from discovery of applications (think assessment solutions like Lakeside SysTrack, Citrix AppDNA, or Liquidware Labs Stratusphere) to purchasing additional software or licenses, to training users, to managing applications and users after they reach their new home.

Also keep in mind that there are often one-time fees that your DaaS provider will charge you to do specific engineering work to get your desktops into their cloud. This could be for things like hooking up your Active Directory to their cloud, setting up shares and file servers, and optimizing your base disk image for their environment. Costs are hard to pin down because what needs to be done varies from customer to customer, but roughly speaking these one-time fees could cost you from $5 to $50 per user.

So that pretty much wraps up the business end of DaaS. In the past few chapters, we've looked at licensing, costs, advantages, and disadvantages. The stuff that makes IT staff's heads spin is over, and now it's time to move into the technology.

10. How to Pick a Windows Platform

One of the big decisions you have to make when designing your DaaS environment is what Windows platform you're going to use for the desktops you rent from your provider. When we talk about platform, most people immediately think we're talking about something like Windows 7 versus Windows 8. But there's an even bigger issue here. As we discussed previously, Microsoft does not allow for the rental of Windows desktop OS licenses. The only Windows licenses you can rent are Windows *Server* licenses. So right off the bat you have to think about whether you want your DaaS desktops to run on a desktop platform (Windows 7, Windows 8.1, etc.) or a server platform (Windows Server 2008 R2, Server 2012, etc.).

Windows Server Versus Windows Desktop

If you're confused by the issue, think of it like this: If you got a brand new empty laptop and had to install Windows on it, you could install Windows 8.1 or you could install Windows Server 2012 R2. We're not talking about using your laptop as an Exchange Server or anything—we're talking about the fact that Windows Server looks and feels a lot like a Windows desktop, and if you wanted to you could install the Windows Server OS on your laptop and use it like a regular laptop. As we mentioned earlier, you could even install the Windows Desktop Experience feature with all its GPU-enhanced goodness. You could enable the desktop indexing service and disable and remove all the server stuff you don't need. Really you can make Windows Server look and feel a lot like a Windows desktop.

Why would you want to do that? This is all thanks to Microsoft's ludicrous licensing policies and the fact that they don't allow DaaS providers to provide Windows desktop licenses on a rental basis. So if you're shopping around for a DaaS provider and they tell you that their price includes the required Windows licenses, guess what? They're providing you with a Windows Server desktop instead of a "real" Windows 7 or 8 desktop.

The million-dollar question is, "Okay, so what? Does that matter?"

It's hard to say. In most cases it doesn't. The DaaS provider can make Windows Server look just like Windows desktop. They can still give each user his or her own virtual machine so you only have one user per desktop (err, server), and really that's fine.

To be clear, not every DaaS desktop is based on Windows Server. Remember that Microsoft *does* allow external third-party hosting companies (i.e., DaaS providers) to host real Windows desktop machines as long as the customer is paying for Software Assurance (SA) or Virtual Desktop Access (VDA) and the provider is set up such that they can dedicate hardware to the customer. So if you have an agreement with Microsoft under which the users you want to host in the DaaS environment are covered by SA or

VDA, your DaaS provider can host real Windows 7 or 8 desktops for you as long as you provide the licenses. As we said previously, this bring-your-own-license (BYOL) game is pretty common in the DaaS world.

In the grand scheme of things, whether you use DaaS desktops running on Windows 7 or 8 with BYOL or you pay your DaaS provider for Windows Server-based desktops doesn't really make too much of a difference from a technical standpoint. Again, in most cases it comes down to cost. If you don't have SA, you'll probably be shocked by the price Microsoft charges for it, so usually in those cases it makes sense to just pay the DaaS provider for the rental of Windows Server licenses.

On the other hand, if you're paying for SA now, you might be able to save a few dollars a month per user if you go the BYOL route, since the provider wouldn't have to pay for the licenses.

Single-user Windows Server Versus Remote Desktop Session Host

The question about Windows Server desktops versus real Windows 7 or 8 desktops is only part of the conversation when it comes to the Windows platform a DaaS provider uses. The other part of it is single-user Windows Server versus multiple users per server with Remote Desktop Session Host (RDSH).

You might know that RDSH, a Microsoft Windows Server technology, lets multiple users run desktops on the same server at the same time, with each user in a unique session. RDSH is the modern name for the technology that was originally known as Terminal Server (TS), and it's also the name of the technology that a lot of people refer to as server-based computing (SBC). So for the purposes of this book, RDSH = SBC = TS. RDSH is the technology on which Citrix MetaFrame and Citrix XenApp are based, as well as other solutions like Dell vWorkspace.

Back in the days before server virtualization, RDSH was extremely popular because it would allow a high density of users per server. A single RDSH server could easily run 100 or more simultaneous user sessions. The catch was that all the users were using the same copy of Windows at the same time, and while user profiles allowed each user to have different settings and wallpapers and stuff, RDSH worked best when the users were all fairly similar. (In later years we started using app virtualization technologies like Microsoft App-V and VMware ThinApp to put different applications in different sessions, but even so, RDSH was best when the users were similar-ish to each other.)

Nowadays you have virtualization and hypervisors, so the decision as to whether you should use RDSH is not as cut-and-dried. For example, if you have 100 users who all need a Windows desktop, what's better—a single VM running RDSH with 100 users sharing that VM, or 100 separate VMs with one user each? Isolating each user in his or her own VM has some benefits versus 100 users in one VM, but 100 users each in a separate VM means you're running 100 VMs! Even with the latest advances in hypervisor technology, you're still going to need more hardware to run 100 single-user VMs as opposed to running a 100 user sessions in a single VM.

The other issue with RDSH is that it can be finicky at times. Even though it's been around since the Terminal Server days of the 1990s, there are still some apps that don't quite work right when multiple users use them at once on the same machine. RDSH is also perceived as being less secure than isolating all your users onto separate VMs. After all, imagine you have a competitor renting desktops from the same DaaS provider as you. What would you be more comfortable with: putting your users in their own sessions on the same RDSH server as your competitor, or having your users isolated onto their own VMs that are separate from your competitor's VMs?

Then again, it all comes down to price. Since you can fit more users on RDSH servers than you can on environments where each user has his own VM, DaaS offerings based on RDSH's session per user are typically less expensive than solutions that are one VM per user.

Picking Your Windows Platform

Based on the various Windows platform options, you'll find that the "Windows desktop" a DaaS provider is selling could be any one of the following options:

- A single VM per user, running a "real" desktop OS like Windows 7 or 8.1.

- A single VM per user, running a server OS like Windows Server 2008 R2 or Server 2012 dressed up to look like a desktop OS.

- A session per user, with multiple users per server (or virtual server), running on Windows Server RDSH.

You'll have to read the technical documentation or ask your DaaS provider about which options they offer. Some providers offer all three options (at different price points), while others offer only one or two. The confusing thing is that most providers refer to all three of these options collectively as Windows desktops or even VDI, so you need to make sure you find out what they're really offering instead of just assuming, "Oh, since they're calling it VDI, it must be the first option."

To be clear, it's impossible to say whether any of these is bad or good, or whether any of them is really better than the other, because it all depends on what you're trying to do and, frankly, what your DaaS provider offers. Most important is that from the users' standpoint, there is no functional difference between any of the three options. They click on a button and see their desktop, their wallpaper, and their Start button. They shouldn't care (or even know) which platform option you choose for them, because from their standpoint it doesn't matter.

In fact, there was a controversy a few years ago where a DaaS provider was selling "VDI desktops" that were actually Windows Server VMs disguised to look like Windows 7 desktops. Someone called them out on Twitter and then the whole industry started digging into those desktops to try to prove they were server desktops and not Windows 7 desktops. The two of us were thinking,

"Okay, so if it's taking a hundred geeks three days to figure this out, who really cares?" If an IT geek can't immediately know, why should anyone care? Why should the user care? (We still think that today, frankly.)

That said, let's run through some advantages and disadvantages of each of the three platform options. These may or may not apply to you, and again, our belief is that in a lot of cases it doesn't even matter, but here goes.

Single VM per user (desktop OS)

This is the traditional (if we can use such a word) VDI. The OS is a normal desktop OS like Windows 7 or Windows 8.1, and each user's desktop runs in its own VM. Because this is the regular desktop OS, it's theoretically the preferred route. Running your DaaS desktops on Windows 7 or 8.1 is nice because you can have the exact same OS in there as you have on your traditional laptops and desktops. That means you have the exact same patches, update cycles, and support processes—everything is just the same.

The problem again is the fact that Microsoft does not allow DaaS providers to rent out these desktop OS licenses. So the only way you can get this is if you pay Microsoft for the ridiculously expensive SA or VDA licenses for your desktops. If you already do that, great! But if you don't, paying for SA just to get Windows desktop OSes in your DaaS is probably not worth it.

Single VM per user (server OS)

This option is exactly like the previous option except the OS running in the desktop VMs is a copy of Windows Server dressed up (or disguised, if you want to be snarky) to look like a Windows client desktop.

This is probably fine for 99.99% of the world, but as we said earlier, every once in awhile we find some crazy (typically internally developed) application that was written for the Windows desktop that just won't run on a server OS. So even though there's no real difference, it's like that app says, "Am I on a Windows desktop?

No? AAAAAHHHHHHH!!!!! <crash>" But that should be something you can find out pretty quickly in your testing.

Some people don't like the "server OS as a desktop" thing simply because Microsoft doesn't allow for desktop license rentals. We argued just now that they're effectively the same, but the counterargument is, "If they're the same, then why does Microsoft license them differently?" It's a fair point in some ways, though questioning Microsoft's licensing is like questioning God, and no good can come from that.

So for most of the world, running your desktops on a server OS disguised as a desktop should be fine. It really is just a licensing thing, and barring some Nadella (Microsoft CEO) miracle from on high, we don't see this changing anytime soon.

Multiple user sessions per VM (server OS plus RDSH)

Running multiple users on a single server via RDSH has one major advantage: price. Even in 2014, it takes less hardware to run a session than it does a full VM. We talked about how the beauty of DaaS is that you don't have to sully yourself with the technical details of your provider's platform, but we mention the hardware thing here because if your DaaS provider is offering you an RDSH-based session per user, it should be cheaper than one of the first two VM-per-user options above.

The biggest gotcha here is that since you have a bunch of users running on the same VM, one mistake has the potential to break a lot of users all at once. This isn't really a problem from a security standpoint—Microsoft has had 15-plus years of Terminal Server/RDSH to work out those bugs—but we occasionally hear of situations where an admin replaces a DLL or updates a plugin or something for one user that ends up breaking everyone else.

The other limitation to RDSH is that since all the users share the same Windows Server, they're all sharing the same base Windows image. So you have non-persistent desktops by default. (Which makes sense. With RDSH, you can't practically allow one user to install a new application because that app would be in the base server image, which would apply to all the users on that server.)

So if your desktop plans allow for shared, non-persistent images, this session-per-user RDSH model might be a great way to get DaaS for a bit less money. But if you need fully personal, persistent disk images, you'll have to go with one of the first two VM-per-user options. (And if you have no idea about which type of image you need, then read on, because the entire next chapter is about image management.)

Full Desktops Versus Single Applications

Another decision you'll have to make is whether your DaaS users will connect to full remote desktops or single Windows applications. The full desktop option means that when your users connect to the DaaS desktop, they see a full Windows desktop, complete with a wall paper image, a task bar, and a Start button. Users navigate the remote Start menu to launch applications, and when they Alt+Tab between multiple running apps, they're switching between apps in the remote desktop.

The full desktop option is the best for scenarios when your DaaS desktop will be the primary desktop your users use, or when you have multiple applications in your DaaS environment and you want to ensure that your users can easily switch between them. This is the option that people envision when they think about DaaS.

The other option is for your users to just connect to single remote Windows applications. (This is similar to what Citrix calls published applications, or like VMware Fusion's Unity or Parallels Desktop's Coherence modes.) When connecting to a single app, users do *not* see the full remote desktop. No wallpaper. No task bar. No Start button. Instead they click on an application link or icon and poof!—their Windows application appears right in front of them.

From a technology standpoint, when users only connect to a single application, it's still DaaS. That app is still running on the Windows desktop in the DaaS provider's data center. The authentication, login script, and user profile all work in the same way. The only difference is that the desktop background and Windows elements are "hidden" from the user, so the user only sees the actual application window. (Oftentimes these environments are configured so that when the user closes the application, the remote Windows session is automatically logged out and disconnected.)

Connecting to seamless Windows applications is great for environments where you only have a few Windows applications you'd like to deliver via DaaS to existing users who do most of their work locally on their own devices. (Google Chromebook users are good candidates for this. Your users can probably do 99% of their work via web apps through the Chrome browser, and then you can use these DaaS-based remote Windows applications for the few situations where users need the full Windows desktop applications.)

Most of the DaaS hosting providers have options where you can provide these seamless Windows applications to your users instead of full remote desktops. (In most cases it can be done with the multi-user RDSH shared-session servers, which is typically cheaper than full-on VDI desktops.) There are also some DaaS providers (such as Mainframe2, Amazon Web Services' AppStream, and possibly Microsoft's future Mohoro project, which we'll discuss later) that are dedicated to only providing single Windows applications from the cloud instead of full remote desktops.

So for your DaaS environment, it makes sense to look at how many and what type of Windows applications your users need. It may work out that you can provide just the Windows applications without the rest of the desktop.

11. Desktop and Image Management

In this chapter we're going to dig into the management aspects of your DaaS environment. We've decided to combine desktop management and image management, since the two concepts are so tightly interconnected.

Desktop Management in a DaaS Environment

As we've mentioned several times, deciding to outsource your VDI environment to a DaaS provider does *not* mean that the DaaS provider is going to do all of your desktop management and engineering for you. The DaaS provider's job is to make sure your users can connect to a running copy of Windows. What happens once the users connect is still up to you. That means that even with DaaS, you're in charge of both desktop engineering and desktop management.

At this point you might be thinking, "But I want to outsource everything! I don't want to think about desktops ever again!" The good news is that if you're looking for that, there are plenty of companies that will do that for you. The bad news is that it will cost you. How much it will cost will depend on what exactly you want them to do, but suffice it to say you're looking at a lot more than the "dollar a day" many DaaS providers quote for the price of operating desktops.

If you decide that the price is worth it and you want to outsource the entire engineering and management of your desktops, you'll probably need to shop around for something more like an MSP (managed service provider) or "desktop outsourcing" rather than a DaaS provider, though what exactly you end up with is somewhat an issue of semantics. For example, some companies calling themselves DaaS providers might have add-on options that include the fully outsourced management of your desktops. Other desktop outsourcing companies might offer to manage all of your desktops as they are (as physical machines in your office) rather than having you migrate them to VDI in the provider's environment.

The important thing to keep in mind is that DaaS is VDI, and VDI is just a form factor option. VDI (and therefore DaaS) is not about desktop management, so in most cases if you choose DaaS, that doesn't change how you manage your desktops or who's responsible for them. And if you choose to outsource the management of your desktops, that's a separate business decision from what form factor (desktop, laptop, or VDI) your desktops are.

This means that when it comes to desktop form factors and management options, there are several valid combinations of these possibilities:

- Physical desktops and laptops, managed by you.
- Virtual desktops (VDI) running in your own environment, managed by you.
- Virtual desktops (VDI) running in someone else's environment (DaaS), managed by you.
- Physical desktops and laptops, managed by someone else.

- Virtual desktops (VDI) running in your own environment, managed by someone else.
- Virtual desktops (VDI) running in someone else's environment (DaaS), managed by someone else.

Again, keep in mind that you don't need to choose a single option for everyone in your company. You might have physical desktops in your main office and DaaS desktops for your remote users, all managed by you. And then you might also choose DaaS desktops managed by someone else for a branch office in another country.

Of course the six options listed above are just representative examples of how you can think about the relationship between desktop form factor and desktop management. In the real world, the line is much wider and more gray.

For example, what exactly does "desktop management" mean? We could probably come up with a list of desktop management tasks that's 200 items long (patching, application installation, mapping printers, configuring Outlook, help desk, troubleshooting, and so on). When shopping around for DaaS providers, it's not like it's an either/or where it's either you have to do all 200 things or the provider does all 200. In most cases the DaaS provider does certain things (they apply Windows patches, they update the antivirus software) while you do other things (you install new applications, you set up printers).

So this is why we say that who manages your desktops comes down to semantics. Again, using our (arbitrary) 200 desktop management tasks, do you do 190 and the DaaS provider does 10? Do you do 150 and they do 50? Is it 120-80, 100-100, 50-100, 0-200? And at what point do you say "I'm managing my desktops" versus "They're managing my desktops?" (And, frankly, does the distinction even matter?)

The lines blur even more when you add additional service providers into the mix. If you want to "fully" outsource the management of your VDI desktops, you might find that the company who manages your desktops is separate from the DaaS provider, so you might end up with a task breakdown of 10-180-10. (You add and delete users; your outsourcer does all the installation, man-

112 • DESKTOPS AS A SERVICE

agement, and support; and your DaaS provider keeps the antivirus up to date.)

Regardless of who actually performs each task, the most complex part of DaaS management is the management of the disk images used for your remote desktops. So let's take a look at that first.

Disk Image Management

One of the big desktop management tasks in traditional desktop environments that also applies to VDI and DaaS is image management. Image management is how you're creating and maintaining the disk images for your desktop users.

This has evolved quite a bit over the past few decades. In the old days we would buy a desktop PC from the vendor and it would have Windows preinstalled. Then we'd spend a few hours installing the apps the user needed, adding the desktop to the domain, and setting up the user's mail and user profile, and we'd be all set! We'd deliver the new desktop to the user's desk (by putting it on a cart and pushing it down the hall), answer any questions he or she had, cross our fingers, and move on to the next desktop.

In those environments, we fixed things as they broke, updated apps as needed, and, if things got really bad, wiped the desktop and started over. (Wiping the desktop involved copying off the user's data, reformatting the hard drive, setting up everything from scratch again, and copying the data back on—pretty much everything you do on your mom's Packard Bell when you go home for the holidays.)

That was fine for the early years but proved to be problematic for enterprises. In addition to taking a lot of time, manual computer builds meant that no two PCs in the company were exactly the same, and manually updating software on dozens of PCs took forever and was super-boring.

The next evolutionary step from there was for us to create a single master disk image that we could use for multiple PCs. Typically we'd pick one PC and install a fresh copy of Windows along with all of the software and configurations that most users needed. Then we'd use software (or a disk duplicating machine) to take an image (or snapshot) of our master computer. From that point on, whenever we got new PCs in, we'd just copy our image (complete with all of our default settings and applications) onto the new PC. Once that was done, we only had to do a few last-minute things to customize the image for that specific user (add the machine to the domain, set up email, and make sure the user could access his or her files). Using a master image got us maybe 90% of the way there, so manually configuring and installing the last 10% meant that we could get a new PC out to the user much quicker than when we manually installed everything. It was also nice for users who broke things, since we could simply back up their files and re-image their PC at their desk with our BartPE disk or whatever. After that, we'd restore their data and we'd be all set!

Using a master image was great for building or (rebuilding) PCs, but it didn't help us maintain the images once they were out in the field. How did we apply service packs, hotfixes, and application updates to hundreds of desktops?

One option was to simply re-image all of our PCs every so often. Some companies did this as often as every three months, and it certainly was an effective way to keep everything up to date. The downside is that whenever we re-imaged a PC, we blew away any changes the user had made. While that was a good thing in terms of keeping the PCs fresh and working well, it was bad in that users would lose any of the applications they had installed on their own. Sure, we could easily back up their My Documents folder and other files, but that still wouldn't protect user-installed apps and many other customizations they made. Plus, if there were multiple types of PCs on the floor (and there were), that meant multiple images. Also, many companies had department-specific images with different applications on each one, so that led to different images for each type of PC in each department, each of which had to be maintained so that it could be used to re-image all the desktops. Yikes!

The way that most companies dealt with this was to use some kind of remote software "push" product, like Microsoft Systems Management Server (now called System Center Configuration Manager), Altiris' Client Management Suite, LANDesk, or some similar product. These software distribution products allowed us to build software installation and update scripts that we could push out to our users. So when a new service pack came out, we could push it out at night to hundreds of computers at once.

The upside to remote software distribution was that we didn't have to manually visit all those desktops. It was also nice that we could keep the desktops up to date without having to re-image them, meaning our users wouldn't lose anything they'd installed on their own after receiving our initial image. The downside to these software distribution tools was that they required a lot of expertise around how to write the software installation scripts, and the scripts didn't always work right. It seemed like we were always running around the day after a big update to manually fix the computers that didn't complete the overnight installation properly.

If you fast-forward to today's desktop environments, we find that even 10 to 20 years later, the basic concept of imaging PCs and laptops hasn't changed much. Most companies typically create a baseline master image that is used as the default starting point for their desktops, and then once it's deployed, they use software distribution tools to keep that image up to date. And, still, every once in awhile a particular desktop gets so broken that they decide to just re-image it back to its "golden" state rather than trying to figure out why it didn't work.

Understanding persistent and non-persistent images

We already talked a bit in the opening of this book about image management in VDI environments and how there's a big conversation around whether you should use persistent or non-persistent disk images. The technical difference is that persistent images "persist" from session to session, so anything users change one day will be there the next time they log in. A non-persistent image means that the image is discarded from time to time (typically each time the user logs off), so when the user logs on again, he or she gets a brand new fresh image.

(Persistent images are also referred to as personal or one-to-one images, since each user has his or her own image, while non-persistent images are also called shared or pooled images, since a single base-level image is used by multiple users.) When people who are new to VDI hear about the differences between non-persistent and persistent images, they immediately think that non-persistent images are awesome. After all, who *wouldn't* want their users to have a brand new fresh disk image every time they log in? This would mean that any crazy things the user does, installs, downloads, or otherwise breaks will instantly be wiped clean the next time he or she logs in!

Furthermore, updates are very easy with non-persistent images. Since non-persistent images are thrown away after they're used, you typically have to create only a single master image that's used for all your users. (Think of the master image as a template. Users basically get a temporary image based on the master template when they log in, and then when they log out, that temporary image is deleted. The next time they log in they get a brand new temporary copy.) Deploying mass updates via non-persistent images is as simple as an administrator booting up a virtual machine based on the master image, making the changes (patches, updates, etc.) to that image, and then re-saving it as the new master template. From that point forward, anytime users log in, they get a temporary image based on the new template, and voila! You've now "deployed" your changes to dozens or even hundreds of users!

From a theoretical standpoint, non-persistent images seem awesome. They're always fresh, and it's simple to update thousands of desktops at once. The downside to non-persistent images is that they are a big departure from the way traditional (non-VDI) desktop computing works, since normal desktops and laptops are almost always persistent. After all, regular laptops and desktop PCs have local hard drives in them. When you shut them off one day, the computer boots up from the same hard drive the next day. Applying a non-persistent image model to traditional desktops is certainly possible, but it would be analogous to re-imaging every computer every time it was booted up. (How would that even be done? You'd have to PXE boot to a Ghost Server or use a product like Faronics Deep Freeze.)

So the reality of traditional desktop computing is that images are persistent. If you want to move from persistent traditional desktops to non-persistent images in your VDI environment, you'd have to answer a lot of questions, such as:

- What do you do about the applications? Sure, you could install applications into your base template image, but what about different groups of users that need different applications? Do you build multiple image templates for different groups? Do you use app virtualization products like Microsoft App-V or VMware ThinApp to stream applications on demand to just the users who need them? What about apps that aren't compatible with app virtualization? Do you use FSLogix Apps to put all the applications in your base image and then hide the apps that certain users don't need?

- How do you handle user-installed apps? In a non-persistent environment, any app that a user installed would be lost when that temporary image was blown away, meaning the app would have "disappeared" overnight. Do you not allow user-installed apps? Do you install every app that every user might need in your base image? Do users request new apps from IT? How do you regression test all those? What about licensing?

- How do you handle user settings and data? Sure, you can use things like roaming profiles and folder redirection, but what if users change things that aren't captured in the standard folders? Do you need a third-party user environment management (UEM) tool?

As we previously discussed in the chapter about VDI, the move from persistent desktops to non-persistent desktops is a really big deal. We believe it's the single biggest reason VDI projects fail. So now that you are designing your DaaS implementation, you have to decide whether you'll use persistent images, non-per-

DESKTOP AND IMAGE MANAGEMENT • 117

sistent images, or a combination of both. After all, even though using DaaS means that the VDI infrastructure design won't cause your project to fail, not appreciating the difficulty of moving from persistent images to shared images can absolutely still cause your DaaS project to end in disaster.

Picking the image type

As we've also mentioned before, we are huge proponents of keeping your VDI desktops (and therefore your DaaS desktops) as similar as possible to your traditional Windows desktops. So, if your traditional desktops are persistent (which they most likely are), your DaaS desktops should also be persistent.

The good news is that with today's storage technologies, building VDI with fully persistent images is absolutely possible without a crazy cost. This is a big difference from a few years ago when 100 persistent VDI desktops would have required 100 separate disk image files, each taxing the storage capacity and performance of the storage system.

But now there are multiple storage vendors doing all sorts of cool things like block-level deduplication and single-instance block-level storage. These are both fancy terms for recent enhancements to storage optimization that mean that, from at least a storage standpoint, it shouldn't matter whether you want VDI desktops based on persistent images or non-persistent images.

The result is that most of today's DaaS providers can offer persistent images (sometimes for the same cost as non-persistent images), so you can make the choice that's best for you from a management standpoint without having to worry about the technology that makes it happen. After all, that's why you're choosing someone else to manage your VDI with DaaS, right?

At this point in the story someone usually interrupts us to tell us that we're crazy: "Persistent images represent the past!" or "Persistent images must die!" All we can say is that we really, really want your DaaS project to be successful. Moving from a traditional desktop to a VDI/DaaS desktop is a huge change, and we don't want to add additional risk to the project by also trying to move from persistent images to non-persistent images. That just seems like too much to bite off all at once.

Another funny objection people have to our recommendation to keep doing persistent disk images is, "But how are you going to manage all those things?" We answer simply, "Why don't you just keep doing what you've been doing all along?" You've been using persistent images for 20 years, so if you're managing them with Windows Update and SCCM and manual intervention here and there, why wouldn't you just keep on doing that?

"But," the naysayers argue, "then you're missing the opportunity to change the way you manage your desktops! Aren't VDI and DaaS all about making things *easier* to manage?" Our answer to that is, "No, VDI and DaaS are about user flexibility, not management." At the risk of sounding like a broken record, do not move to VDI or DaaS if you're just looking for a better way to manage Windows. Move to VDI or DaaS because you want to increase the flexibility for your users, or because you want to make it easier for users to work from anywhere and from any device, or because you want to reign in control on remote workers and contractors. Trying to move to VDI or DaaS at the same time that you switch your fundamental Windows management style is a recipe for disaster.

Throughout all this, remember that you don't have to make this an all-or-nothing approach. You might have some groups of users that truly are very similar to each other. They might all use the same apps, they might never need to install new apps, and they might be fine with all their customizations saved in roaming profiles. In those cases it might make sense for all of them to share the same master image template and use desktops in a non-persistent way.

But if you have other users who are used to having admin rights and doing whatever they want, trust us, you want to keep them on persistent images as you move them to VDI or DaaS.

Creating your master image template

Regardless of whether you choose persistent or non-persistent images, at some point you'll have to create that initial master (or set of masters) template image. If you're using persistent images, this will be the initial image template that's used to create the persistent image each user will "own" a permanent copy of moving forward. If you're using non-persistent images, this will be the template that is used as the temporary image that each user gets a fresh copy of each time he or she connects.

The good news is that master image template creation is an area where your DaaS providers can help you. Most DaaS providers either have baseline template images they can give you that you can customize, or they have best practices to walk you through how to create a template image that works with their DaaS system. Creating a master image template is certainly more of an art than a science, and in fact, we could probably write an entire book on the subject, but the basic things you have to do are fairly straightforward:

- Install the Windows OS and all of its patches.
- Install all the Windows applications you'd like all your users to use.
- Make any registry or configuration customizations that will be common for all users.
- Install any software agents your DaaS provider needs for the disk image to hook into their DaaS system (Citrix Virtual Desktop Agent, VMware View Agent, etc.).
- Install any custom drivers the DaaS provider needs for their platform (GPU, etc.).
- Clean up any user-level customizations that might have been installed when you were installing your apps. For example, if you install Microsoft Office into your base image, you don't want it to have your name embedded as the last person who edited every document.
- Configure your Windows licensing so the desktops don't have to be "activated" each time they're powered on.

- Disable all the auto-update functions of the OS and individual applications. This is especially true for non-persistent desktops. Since these images are thrown away after they're used, an application that tries to update itself will do it again and again and again every time it's used.
- Configure folder redirection or point certain registry keys to the appropriate partitions. (Some DaaS providers point all temp files and the paging file to the D: drive, or maybe they want My Documents pointed to a per-user volume, etc.)
- Remove and clean up any temp files that were left during the installation process.

As we said, image template creation is an art in itself, and there are dozens of websites, tools, hints, and tips out there for how to create a good image. This is definitely a case where having more experience helps, and you will absolutely make mistakes your first time. The key here is to lean on your DaaS provider for guidance. They've been through it before and can help you. (Even if you're an expert on image creation and you have an image that's ready to go, you'll still need your provider's help to make sure you install the drivers and agents they need for your image to work in their DaaS system.)

Dividing the Management Between You and the DaaS Provider

By now we hope that it's painfully clear that moving to DaaS does not automatically change the way you manage your desktops. In most cases your DaaS provider does nothing more than provide the VDI infrastructure on which your desktops run—all the management of those desktops typically falls to you.

That said, if you read the marketing materials from most DaaS providers, they talk about how they provide you with a "fully managed desktop." So what gives?

Well, the proverbial devil is in the details. Some DaaS providers use the term "fully managed" to describe the fact that they're managing the VDI that's powering your desktops. So they're fully managing the VDI platform, the servers, the storage, the network, and so on. Other providers might handle the patching of the Windows OS while leaving the applications to you. Still others might handle the management of some baseline applications like Microsoft Office, a PDF viewer, and antivirus, while everything else is up to you. And still others might handle the deployment of any apps that have MSI installers, but you do everything else. Again, there are no standards here, so you need to ask.

The only thing we can definitively say is that you get what you pay for. If you find a DaaS provider that's offering desktops for $30 per user per month, it's safe to assume that they're not going to do too much inside your desktops. On the other hand, if you're paying $200 per desktop per month, we'd hope you're getting something more than the basics for that price!

In doing the research for this book, we talked to as many DaaS providers as would talk to us, and we scoured the websites of every other one we could find. If we were to summarize everything into a single haiku, we'd write,

Many DaaS providers.
Services vary widely.
So does the cost.

Seriously, there are providers out there selling desktops for $9.99 per desktop per month. OnLive—which you might remember as the online gaming provider who was violating Microsoft's licensing agreements by providing desktops—now has plans even cheaper than that. One where the desktops are accessible "when available" is free, and there's another that guarantees a base-level desktop at $4.99 per month. (These are very limited though. You can't install applications on them, but then again, you get what you pay for.) On the other side of the spectrum, there are DaaS solutions with additional options that put the price over $200 per desktop per month!

That's a pretty big range, but you need to understand that the DaaS model depends on everything in the provider's walls being as identical as possible. Identical equates to predictable, predictable equates to scalable, and scalable equates to profitable. If you want to go against the grain, that's on you to manage and support. If DaaS companies (or even MSPs) took on all the customization work as part of the base fee, they'd never make any money. Sure, they can deliver email and file access as part of that offering, but that's because almost everyone does it the same way. If you asked them about how they do their desktops, they'd all be a little different. Just know that the more flexibility you need, the more the work will be on your plate.

We looked into the causes for the cost variation across DaaS providers and found large differences among the services that various providers offered at varying price points. For example, we found some providers who would:

- Apply Microsoft Windows patches to the base image.
- Perform hourly or daily backups.
- Have "hot spare" desktops on standby in other geographical regions.
- Create, optimize, or maintain your Windows disk images.
- Provide the Microsoft Windows licenses.
- Guarantee that your data is in a certain locality.
- Guarantee that you would not share any hardware with any other customers.
- Meet certain regulatory or security requirements (such as ISO 27001, FIPS 140-2, or SSAE 16).
- Install custom apps based on MSIs.
- Install any custom apps you want.
- Provide provisioning and deprovisioning.
- Refresh desktops back to the default state.

- Give you a control panel where you can set up users, reset desktops, etc.
- Provide licenses for, install, and maintain certain applications. (Microsoft Office and antivirus are the two most popular.)
- Host your email, collaboration, and file-sharing environments.

This is just a partial list, but it gives you an idea of the types of offerings and add-on services that are available from your DaaS provider. Many of these are fairly self-explanatory, but some of them require a bit deeper look.

Administration and management

If your DaaS provider tells you that they provide administration and management of your desktops, what exactly does that mean? Will they notify you before they touch your desktops? Do they only do things that you ask them to? Which, if that's the case, that's kind of bad, right? It's like you have to call the provider every time you want to do something? Then why don't you just do it yourself and save the hassle of asking the provider to do it?

Of course on the other hand, if they're being proactive and doing things without you having to ask, that means they're messing with "your" desktops whenever they want. Would you be comfortable with that? Who at the DaaS provider has administrative rights? If you administer your own servers, can the DaaS provider get back admin rights if they wanted? Which exact parts of your environment are under the control of the DaaS provider?

User-installed applications

If the DaaS provider is providing support for applications, will they also let you install your own applications? Do they let your users install their own applications? What happens if one of the applications you install breaks one of their apps? What if one of the DaaS provider's updates breaks one of your user-installed apps?

Patching

Who does patching? Patching of what? The OS? The applications? Can you ask the DaaS provider not to patch your images? But what if there's a critical patch? Can they force you to do it? Can they go around you?

Antivirus

Whose antivirus is it? What options are used? Can you change those options? Can you run your own antivirus so it matches the rest of your environment?

Backups

What is backed up? Can you add more to the list of what's backed up? Can you back up less? Can you turn backup off all together? How often is it backed up? Can you change that? Can you restore just certain files? Can you do restores? Can the user? Or do you have to contact the DaaS provider? If you leave the DaaS provider, will they delete your backups? Can they prove it?

Performance

What happens if the DaaS desktops don't perform as well as you wanted? Who troubleshoots that? Will the provider proactively notify you of poor performance, or will they wait until a user calls to complain? (By the way, that user is calling you, not the DaaS provider!)

User management

Who creates users? Who removes them? Who resets their passwords? Who changes their group memberships? Can users update their own metadata? (Odds are that this is the exact same process that you use today, but it all depends on how authentication is handled.)

Summary of DaaS Management

We understand this chapter poses more questions than answers. That's the unfortunate reality, since desktop computing environments vary widely from company to company. All we can do is help you ask the questions about your current environment that you need to think about as you're shopping around for DaaS providers.

Then as you're doing that, keep the two most important points of this chapter in mind:

- Moving a desktop from your office to the DaaS cloud is just a physical form factor change. You can choose to also change the way you manage your desktop at the same time as your move, but do so with the understanding that you increase the risk of failure, which could jeopardize your whole DaaS project.

- The specific tasks the DaaS provider does vary greatly among different providers and price points. The main thing that's common though is that while the provider might handle some of the lower-level tasks, many of the desktop management activities you've been doing for the past ten or twenty years will be things you'll still have to do in your new DaaS environment.

12. Data Location and the Network

The next two design elements we're going to dig into have to do with your network and the location of your files, databases, and servers that power the applications your users use on their DaaS desktops. At first you might be thinking these are strange topics to combine into one chapter, but it's easy to see how interrelated they are. If you just move your desktops to the cloud but keep your file servers in your office, your DaaS users (who are in your office) will constantly have to access files in the office from their cloud-based desktops. What will that mean for network bandwidth and desktop performance?

On the flip side of that, what if you move your servers to the cloud? Then you'll have to deal with the remaining on-premises desktops going across the WAN for their files.

Of course there's a lot more to DaaS data and networking than just file servers. You have to figure out where your user profiles will be stored, how you'll handle user authentication, and where other previously internal IT services will live. And on top of all that, you'll have to make sure your network can actually support this increase in traffic while also supporting all the remote display sessions for your DaaS users. Phew!

So let's approach these competing issues like we'd approach any technical design problem. First, we'll lay out all the things you have to think about, and then we'll get into the ways you can incorporate them into your design.

What Do You Have to Think About?

- Whose laws govern my desktops?
- Where do my files live?
- Authentication
- User profiles and settings
- Printing
- Backup
- Other internal IT services and resources

Let's look at each of these.

Whose laws govern my desktops?

One of the beauties of the cloud is the fact that you don't know (or *have* to know) where exactly your data is. All that matters is that it's in the cloud! In most cases that's fine. Do you really care where exactly Google stores the physical ones and zeros that make up your Gmail messages?

For individual consumers, the cloud is great. But for businesses? Not so much. The problem is that different localities have different legal rights and approaches to data privacy and security.

For example, imagine you had some kind of legal issue, such as theft, a subpoena, or employee misconduct that required seizing his or her desktop. In a traditional computing environment, the laws of the state or country that your business is in will dictate the laws that apply to your legal situation. But what if your desktops have been outsourced to a DaaS provider in another state or country? Whose laws apply there?

What if you have proof that someone is spying on your desktops or stealing your data? Do you have the legal ability to go after the thieves in that locality? Will the local government support you?

Where do my files live?

As we've mentioned several times, a Windows desktop doesn't really *do* anything without applications and files. So once you figure out how your DaaS desktops and applications will work, how will your users get access to all their files?

In your current (pre-DaaS) environment, your users' files are probably sitting on the same file servers they've been on for the past ten years. Your users' H: drives or T: drives or whatever they're known as, along with their My Documents folders, most likely map back to file servers in *your* data center with LAN-speed connections to your desktops. Even if you embrace VDI, RDSH, or traditional desktop PCs and laptops, in your traditional on-premises computing environment, everything is on the same LAN.

So what happens when you move to DaaS? If you don't change your file server structure, your users will have to open and save all their files across the WAN. What will that do for their user experience? (Hint: It's not pretty.)

People's gut reactions are typically to just move all their file servers to the cloud too. Most DaaS providers also have options for file server hosting (or IaaS or PaaS options where you can build your own file servers), and if you've accepted the risks of moving your desktops to that DaaS provider, then you probably wouldn't mind moving your file servers there too.

But before you go too far in the thought process, remember that not all of your users are candidates for DaaS. Since DaaS is governed by the same use cases as VDI, there is a large quantity of users in your company who will likely keep their laptops or desktop PCs after the low-hanging fruit machines are raptured away into the cloud.

The good news is that you might have solved this problem already. If you have laptop users who access files from outside your office or a small branch office site with users who need access to the same files as users in your main office, just do whatever you're doing for them for your DaaS users.

If you're not sure what to do, a typical "evolution" happens like this:

The first step is you move some of your users' desktops to your DaaS provider and you just use your existing VPN to map network drives back to file servers in your office. That certainly works, though it's often not the most ideal scenario, as it doesn't lead to the best user experience.

The next step is to figure out if there are some files that are accessed exclusively (or mostly) from your DaaS users. For example, you might have a file server full of users' home drives (My Documents, etc.) in your office, but the users you move to DaaS might never run a desktop in your office again. So why are their files still there? In that case the next step is to move the DaaS users' home drives to your DaaS provider. Again, some providers offer file servers as a service, others might give you an empty Windows server you can configure however you want, and still others might just give you a blank virtual machine and tell you to go nuts.

Once your DaaS users' home drives are in the cloud, next you can look at the shared files they'll access. If you're using DaaS to outsource entire departments or remote offices, it probably makes sense to put those departments' file shares and collaboration servers in the cloud as well.

What's not as clear-cut is what you should do with the file shares that are used by both DaaS users and your on-premises users. Again, this is a case where you can look at what you do for your other branch offices and do that for your DaaS users. If it's just a few users or occasional use, you might be able to get away with just remotely accessing those files from your on-premises servers.

If that proves to be too slow, the next thing to consider is some type of WAN acceleration or caching appliance—typically available as a pair of virtual appliances, one of which you install on-premises and the other in your DaaS provider's cloud. You can check out vendors like Citrix, Riverbed, Silver Peak, and Blue Coat.

Most of these vendors have virtual versions you can pay for by the month, so they fit nicely into your DaaS funding model. (Heck, your DaaS provider might already have a partnership in place with a vendor that has a solution preconfigured and ready to go.)

In most cases those WAN accelerators should work fine, but if you're still having problems, you can look into actually replicating your on-premises file shares to your DaaS provider's environment. You can do this out of the box with Windows' Distributed File System or go for one of the many third-party options.

The last thing we should mention about file shares is that now might be a good time to re-think how you're using them in general. For example, many companies are considering migrating away from on-premises Windows-based file shares protected by VPNs to cloud-based solutions like Dropbox and Box. What's interesting is that these migrations haven't typically come from IT. Rather, they came in via the consumerization route whereby individual users started using them one by one until pretty soon the official file shares were used only by HR. It's only a matter of time until these solutions become the standard way files are shared instead of the exception to the norm.

The new-style cloud-based file syncing solutions (of which there are dozens and dozens) provide a lot of advantages over traditional file shares, including the fact that they work from mobile devices and sync with desktops for fast local access to all types of files. So for DaaS environments, these are great because it doesn't matter whether a user is on-premises or in the cloud—the files are all accessed in the same way. And since you're already comfortable with the cloud—after all, this is a book about DaaS—now's a good time to switch your files over too!

Authentication

Since DaaS users are corporate users, you'll probably want to have a company-controlled way to dictate which users can log in to the DaaS system and a way to remove or lock the accounts of users once they leave the company.

For very small environments, this might be something that can be provided as a standalone solution by your DaaS provider.

As long as you have administrative rights over your users, who cares if they have a username and password for their DaaS desktop that's different from those for their other IT systems. (Your users probably already have fifteen different passwords they're dealing with, so what's another one?)

This won't fly in larger environments, so if you want your users to log in to their DaaS desktops with their domain credentials, you're going to have to figure out how that's happening. Are the DaaS desktops in a separate domain that trusts your corporate domain via a VPN? Is there some sort of identity federation? Do you put a domain controller VM onsite at the provider? Or do the authentication requests simply traverse the wire to a domain controller back in your data center?

Many DaaS customers choose to just put a domain controller at the DaaS provider to help with this LDAP and authentication traffic. (Typically they do so not to minimize the amount of traffic between their data center and the DaaS provider, since the domain controllers still have to replicate and stuff, but rather to help speed along the general use and login times for the desktops.)

User profiles and settings

A big part of any Windows desktop environment is your users' Windows profiles. So how will you handle that for your DaaS desktops?

If you're using persistent disk images, you might not have to worry about user profiles at all, since you could just use local profiles and be all set. (Think about that. The whole point of Windows roaming profiles is that users can log in from any machine and get their own profile. The whole point of DaaS is that users can log in from anywhere and get their own Windows desktop. So with persistent DaaS, the desktop essentially becomes the profile, so you don't have to deal with roaming profiles anymore!) Of course, roaming profiles have the advantage of living on a file server that is backed up. If you abandoned profiles and let the desktop become the profile, you'd need to start backing up your desktops.

If you're using non-persistent desktop images for your DaaS, you probably do need to think about how you're handling your user profiles. Are you using Windows roaming profiles? A third-party tool from AppSense, RES, Tricerat, Scense, Norskale, or Liquidware Labs? Regardless of what you're using, you're going to have to decide where that data is stored and whether you're replicating it between the cloud and your own location.

If you're looking for advice on which option to use, you already know what we're going say: Use whatever you're using in your traditional environment for your DaaS environment!

Printing

If you've never experienced the pain of using RDSH or VDI in the past, you've been blissfully unaware of any of the printing problems that exist when your desktops run in a location that's far away from your printers. Don't worry. We can get you caught up with the "PDF from hell" story. (This is real.)

The PDF from hell is where a user in a Terminal Server (RDSH) session opens an 11 MB PDF file. This PDF causes Adobe Acrobat to consume 80 MB of memory, which seems odd but not impossible, and certainly something you can deal with (even back in 2007, when it was first documented by our friend Jeroen van de Kamp). After browsing the document for a while, the memory usage balloons up to 150 MB. Then when the user prints it, memory usage increases to 216 MB.

Throughout all this, the CPU is spiked at 100% as the user browses the document because, as we all know, Acrobat is awful. Then once the print job starts, the CPU stays pegged at 100% for nearly two minutes! (Keep in mind that this is happening on a Terminal Server, so good luck to everyone else who's trying to work at the same time.) When the CPU finally calms down after the print job has finished processing, you end up with a 741 MB spool file that now needs to be transferred to the printer!

If the desktop processing this PDF is in the cloud and the destination printer is sitting on your desk, that means in addition to spiking the CPU for two minutes, the act of printing causes a 741 MB file to be downloaded across the WAN to your printer. Yikes!

Granted, this is a worst-case scenario caused by a specific PDF file, but it's an accurate illustration of the kind of problems you can run into when printing in remote computing environments like DaaS. Printer spool files are typically much larger than the size of the document you're printing, so where the document is spooled and where it's ultimately printed have huge impacts on your network use.

If you think that sounds terrible (and let us assure you, it is), imagine that scenario with all of your desktops being remote. Since they're running in the cloud and your printers are in your office, printing can become more problematic than ever. Do you move your print server to the cloud? Would that even help?

The good news is there are several third-party printing solutions that address these exact problems. Citrix and VMware have both licensed or built printing optimization technology into their VDI products, and there are standalone third-party printing solutions from companies like ThinPrint, Tricerat, and UniPrint. There are also cloud-based printing solutions that work well in DaaS environments, like Google Cloud Print.

These third-party solutions work by inserting themselves into the print process, optimizing print jobs before sending them to their respective queues. Each works a bit differently. Some require a full version of Windows running on the client side to enumerate printers and receive print jobs, while others install on the print server itself and use a virtual printer driver in the virtual desktop to optimize print data for use over the WAN.

The bottom line is that you'll have to think about printing when you move to your DaaS provider. The good news is there are solutions that can help you.

Backup

We've written many articles in which we've said, "If you have to back up your laptops, you're doing something wrong." Our rationale for this is that all of the important data on a laptop should never be stored only on that laptop. In other words, email is also on the email server, replicated files are on the file server (or in something like Dropbox), applications can be reinstalled from their source, and SaaS apps like Evernote store their data in the cloud.

So we traditionally argue that a well-designed laptop environment doesn't require individual laptop backup, since all the data is already duplicated on some server or in the cloud somewhere.

But when it comes to DaaS, the DaaS desktop *is* that somewhere. So if you're using persistent desktops, and if you're storing your user profiles and your users' My Documents folders locally in those desktop images (or in other partitions at your DaaS provider), then yes, absolutely, you have to back up those DaaS images. The real question is *where* you back up those images and files to. Do you have your DaaS provider back them up to their own location? Do you back them up to another cloud-based provider? Or do you back them up to a location within your own office?

Obviously there's no single (or simple) answer to this—it really depends on what you're trying to protect against and how much you trust your provider. For example, are you backing up your DaaS desktops so you can recover files your users accidentally delete, or are you backing them up in case your DaaS provider goes out of business? If you're just worried about recovering deleted files, you can look to your DaaS provider for a solution that hopefully has a self-service option for users. If you're trying to protect against your DaaS provider going out of business, that means you have to find *another* provider that you trust to meet all your data security and sovereignty requirements, which can be tough. And if you want to back up your DaaS desktops to on-premises storage, you have to deal with all the bandwidth and data transfers associated with that.

None of these scenarios is necessarily a showstopper, but each provides a glimpse of how there's a bit more that goes into backup after your boss comes to you and says, "We have to back up our DaaS desktops."

Other internal IT services and resources

By now you may notice a trend developing, which is once you move to DaaS, anything your users access from their desktops that hasn't also been moved to the cloud will have to be dealt with in some way. Whether that's a VPN connection to your on-premises environment, a replicated version of your service in the DaaS provider's data center, or a whole-hearted replacement of your internal service with a cloud-based equivalent—you're going to have to figure something out. So make a list now, before you start playing with DaaS, so you're prepared when this comes up.

Sizing Your Network to Support DaaS

Now that we've listed out all the various components and services that will consume capacity on your network, let's take a look at how you can design a network that's robust enough to actually handle all of these things.

Determining what type of network connection you need, both in terms of bandwidth and latency to your provider, is not an easy task. Unfortunately we constantly see people's failed attempts to simplify the calculations. They're looking for a straight number they can give their boss, like "100 Kbps per user." In reality, going with a number you got from a book is just as likely to succeed as throwing a dart at a board or just totally pulling a number out of the sky.

Companies struggle with this when deploying straight VDI or RDSH on their own, so you can imagine that throwing in the extra services we just described really messes with the numbers. For example, imagine an environment with 100 desktops. How fast of an internet connection did that office have before DaaS? 15 Mbps? 20 Mbps? Then what happens if the company moves them all to DaaS? Do they need a faster connection because they now have 100 users using a remoting protocol all day? Or do they need a slower connection because all of their internet browsing and file downloads are now between the DaaS provider and the internet instead of between the office and the internet? Or do they need a faster connection because their file shares all have to go across the internet too? Or a slower one because . . .

You get the point. It's not so cut-and-dried, is it?

We're going to provide a framework you can use to think about the network connection you'll need, but the reality is that every environment is different, so all we can really do is give you some advice about how to find a starting point and then try to convince you to test, test, and test.

Once you come up with your first guess, (yeah, guess, not estimate), you can set up a proof of concept, work on the DaaS desktops like a normal user, gauge what kind of connection is needed, and scale it up for a pilot. Then in the pilot phase, you can make more observations, adjust your calculations, cross your fingers, and scale up to production.

So let's begin. The first step is to think about the different types of network traffic you need to understand. We break these into three categories:

- DaaS desktop to end user. (Remoting protocol traffic.)
- Internet traffic from the DaaS desktop and the internet. (The users' web browsing, etc.)
- Data center to data center traffic. (Transfers between the DaaS cloud data center and your on-premises data center, including things like file syncing, user authentication, and application access.)

Let's look at these one by one.

Traffic between the DaaS desktop and the end user

We'll start with the type of traffic that most people think of first when they hear the term VDI or DaaS: the traffic between the cloud-based DaaS desktop and the end user. This is the remoting protocol or remote display protocol traffic that's typically something like Citrix HDX (formerly ICA), Teradici PC-over-IP, Microsoft RemoteFX, or a custom H.264-based protocol.

If you have traditional desktops that you moved to the cloud, this is the traffic that will be going back and forth between the users and their DaaS desktops all day. It includes things like screen images, pixels, video, printing, and audio moving from the remote host to the client, and keystrokes, mouse movements, mic inputs, and webcams moving from the client up to the remote host. It could also include USB redirection traffic in one or both directions, depending on the peripheral.

This remoting traffic is also the most latency-sensitive in your environment, since it affects the actual round trip of a user key press. (The key press is transmitted to the remote host, then the pixel changes are sent back down to the user's screen.)

The good news is that all this traffic isn't necessarily across your office's internet connection. If your users are out in the world instead of in the office, then really this traffic is nothing you need to worry about. (Well, other than making sure that you don't have any home users with dial-up connections.) But for your DaaS users who will be in the office, you'll need to think about how their aggregate use will affect your office's internet connection.

As we mentioned already, a lot has changed since the 1990s era when it was "we need 15 Kbps per user" for ICA traffic in Citrix MetaFrame. But back then you were remoting single Windows desktop applications that were rectangular and gray. You needed to support resolutions of 800×600 or 1024×768, and 256 colors was more than adequate. There were no webcams, VoIP, USB, or 3-D graphics.

Compare that with today. With DaaS, you're *replacing the user's entire desktop* with a new cloud-based desktop. That means that your remoting protocol needs to support *everything* the user does. So today you're talking about one (or two) displays at 1900×1200 with 32-bit color. All of your Windows are transparent and round, and everything is smooth and shaded together. You have USB, microphones, and webcams. Video is now a part of daily life, not a perk. It's a very different world, and compromises will have to be made.

Think about what it takes to remote that entire user environment from a DaaS desktop to the user's client device. The raw math is mind-blowing! If a user has a DaaS desktop with two displays each running at 1900×1200 with 32-bit color, updating every pixel on both screens at 30 times per second requires

2 × 1900 × 1200 × 32 × 30 = 4,377,600,000 bits of data per second, or over 4 Gbps! And that's just for the pixels! It doesn't include audio, USB, printing, and so on. So if that remote protocol is consuming any less than 4 Gbps, there's some kind of compromise going on somewhere.

The good news is that many compromises can be made that users will never notice. For example, not every pixel changes 30 times every second, so the protocols don't need to transmit pixels that don't change. And the protocols can always send fewer than 30 frames per second without the users noticing. Humans are also much more perceptive when it comes to brightness levels (luminance) rather than color (chrominance), so remote protocol vendors can separate these two and send full brightness data down to the users while heavily compressing and slicing color data. (And the list goes on and on—protocol vendors are smart!)

The point is that every single remote desktop experience is going to involve some kind of compromise, and the goal of the people who design them (and the people like you who implement them) is to get the level of compromise low enough that users don't mind. In other words, your goal is to figure out the lowest amount of bandwidth you need per user to deliver a user experience that's still acceptable. (We joke that you just dial down the bandwidth a little bit each day until the users start complaining, then go back to yesterday's setting and lock it in.)

Competition among DaaS providers means that it's going to be hard to get a straight answer from them with regards to bandwidth. Picture each provider as a used car salesman: "What? They're saying 100 Kbps per user? What if I told you we can do it in 90?"

There are constant wars going on in the vendor blogs and at conferences where one vendor will come out and say, "Our protocol used 64% less bandwidth than protocol X for typical tasks." Then of course protocol X's vendor will post a blog response that goes something like, "Our own tests show our protocol uses 40% less bandwidth on a 1 Mbps network versus a 100 Mbps network."

The problem is that tests like these are total BS. Looking at how a protocol (any protocol, not just remote display) uses bandwidth in an unconstrained environment is in no way indicative of how that protocol will perform in a bandwidth-constrained environment. This is why your awesome LAN-based test lab results do *not* translate to awesome WAN-based real-world results.

For remoting protocols, you cannot extrapolate a single user session out to guess how multiple users will behave because user experience and bandwidth consumed are each on a different axis.

Digging into these points a bit more, if you have an unconstrained environment, looking at bandwidth consumption is irrelevant. A good remoting protocol will use as much bandwidth as it possibly can. More data across the wire means a better user experience and less load on the server and client, since they don't have to waste any processing cycles on fancy compression and caching tricks. So when a remote protocol sees a wide-open highway, we say, "Let 'er rip!" In fact, we would say it's a bad thing if a remote protocol *didn't* use more bandwidth when the network was unconstrained. It's like we want to say, "Ummm, hello? There's a wide open network here, so can you please take advantage of it?"

So when the network is unconstrained, that remote protocol *better* deliver an experience that's perfect, because if it doesn't, that means there's some problem with the protocol's ability to scale up!

That said, the unconstrained environment is not realistic for DaaS use cases. A better test would be with multiple users connecting to an actual DaaS environment. And that goes to our second point. Too often people try to figure out the average bandwidth consumption for a remote protocol, but that calculation effort is futile. Sure, it's mathematically possible to work out what the average consumption was per user, per second, per connection, but that number is worthless. You cannot use a calculated average for planning purposes that are not identical.

For example, you might learn that ten users combined consumed an average of 700 Kbps:

- Does that mean that each user averaged 70k?
  Mathematically speaking, yes.

- Does that mean that a single user will have the same quality of experience over a 70k connection?
  No.

- Does that mean that twenty users will have the same quality of experience over a 1,400k connection? *No.*

- Does that mean five users will have the same quality of experience over a 350k connection? *No.*

The big question is which remote protocol provides the best user experience for a certain number of users over a certain bandwidth. The answer to that depends on your users, your applications, your network, and your use case, though to be honest all the current remoting protocols are fine. Seriously, these days they are all awesome. Sure, there are cases where Citrix HDX beats Teradici PC-over-IP and cases where PC-over-IP comes out on top, but especially when compared with a few years ago, things are pretty great nowadays.

Undaunted, people still ask us, "Which remoting protocol is best?" We always answer the same way: "What do you mean 'best?'" Best at what? Best for playing videos? Best for using Microsoft Office? Best in that it uses the least amount of bandwidth? Best because Netflix works through it? Just like how every user has a different definition of what makes a good user experience, every company has a different definition of what makes a remoting protocol best.

Then people say, "Well, I just read this study that shows HDX does . . . " or "Hey, at Benny and Shawn's BriForum session, they said that PC-over-IP . . . " Believe us, doing this advanced protocol analysis in a vacuum without looking at your users, your apps, your network, and your requirements is useless. It's a starting point, not an ending point.

It's like walking into an electronics store and trying to pick the "best" TV from the wall of hundreds. Sure, you can pretty quickly narrow it down based on the type, size, and resolution you want, but even after that there are still probably twenty models to choose from. So when you're in the store trying to pick one, what do you do? You look at color. You squint your eyes and get up close. You watch the same thing on two TVs side by side and ask your friends which image they like better. Then you buy the TV with the "best" image and take it home and hang it on your wall.

And you know what? Once you get that TV home it doesn't make a darn bit of difference which one you chose, because at that point you're not comparing the new TV you bought to the one next to it at the store that you didn't buy. You're comparing the new TV to your old, blurry, glass-tube TV from 1992. The TV you bought or any of the other 19 other options at the store would all look equally awesome to you in your home!

While you were in the store, you were debating which picture elements were most important. Sharpness versus color? Resolution versus black level? But once you got it home, none of that affects the picture quality as much as how dark your room is, whether the sun glare is bouncing off the TV, and how good your input signal is.

The same is true for remoting protocols. You can read all the papers you want and watch twenty years' worth of BriForum session videos online, but at the end of the day what really matters will be how much bandwidth you have, how much latency there is between your users and your DaaS provider, and what exactly your users are doing with their desktops.

The last thing to keep in mind when trying to establish how much remote desktop protocol-related traffic you have is that even if you have VDI today and you *think* you know your way around protocols, keep in mind that all those on-premises VDI users are on an unconstrained LAN connection. Watching their traffic will not help you. (Well, it will, since you'll overbuy your internet connection to the DaaS provider.)

You *can* get some benefit with regards to a baseline by looking at remote users of your VDI environment, but remember remote protocol traffic is just the tip of the iceberg when dealing with DaaS.

Internet traffic from the DaaS desktop and the internet

The next category of network traffic in DaaS environments is best defined as any traffic transmitted from or received by the DaaS desktop that's not part of the remoting protocol and that's not back-end traffic to your data center. In other words, this is the "normal" internet traffic for your users, including web browsing, SaaS apps, downloads, YouTube, Dropbox, and so on.

In the vast majority of cases, this traffic is purely the concern of your DaaS provider. Since it's between the DaaS desktop and the internet, it doesn't touch anything that you're responsible for. Actually a side benefit of DaaS is that oftentimes your DaaS providers have a much bigger pipe to the internet than what you have at your office, so your DaaS desktop users can sort of "virtually" browse the web a lot faster. This doesn't help if they're trying to watch a YouTube video through their DaaS connection, but boy oh boy they can sure download stuff fast to their DaaS desktops!

In some cases, companies will choose to route all of their DaaS desktop-generated internet traffic back to their own data centers. While that sounds crazy to most people, there are scenarios where companies want to do things like scan all desktop Internet traffic for data loss prevention (DLP) purposes or apply website monitoring or security tools. Obviously if you do that, you're taking a 2-times hit on your internet traffic, since everything will go back and forth between the DaaS desktop and your data center, and then your data center and the internet.

If you want to do something like DLP or website monitoring for your DaaS desktops, you don't *have* to route all their internet traffic back through your own data center. Another—perhaps simpler—option would be to install whatever security or DLP software you need in your DaaS provider's data center. You could hook that back into your own environment on the back-end and get the benefits of internet traffic scanning without the detour through your own facility.

Data center to data center traffic

As unpredictable (at least early on) as the remote display protocol traffic could be, your biggest challenge will likely come from the data generated by end-user activity that pulls data from your data center to their desktop in the cloud. This includes file transfer data, which would happen even if you place a file server replica at the DaaS provider (in that case it would be the DFS or sync traffic), data between client/server applications, internal websites, software updates pushed from your office, LDAP and user authentication traffic, application streaming, and so on. Once again, the best way to assess the amount of bandwidth you'll need is best measured during the early phases of your deployment.

As an interesting side note, this is one of the areas where on-premises VDI is better than DaaS. One of the benefits of VDI is that you're relocating your desktops into your data center, which is near all your servers. With DaaS, it's the opposite—you're moving them even farther away from your servers.

Summary

We have two key takeaways from this chapter.

The first is that when it comes to server and service placement, treat your DaaS environment as if it's just another branch office. If you have file servers in your branch office, then put file servers in your DaaS environment. If you have a VPN for user authentication to your branch office, do that for you DaaS. If you have a domain controller and replicated file share for your branch office, do that for your DaaS environment.

The second takeaway is that when it comes to sizing your network connections, it's impossible to know exactly what you'll need up front. The closest you can come is if you have VDI running on-premises now, but even that would change as you extend and replicate parts of your data center to the cloud. The bottom line is that you have to experiment and test, as there are a lot of bits and bytes flying around with DaaS.

13. Security

Back when we talked about the misconceptions of VDI, we mentioned security because a lot of people think that by going to VDI they automatically get more security than what they have with their traditional PCs and laptops. We said that while it is possible to use VDI to deliver a more secure desktop, getting there requires significant planning (in addition to your already significant VDI planning), so in most cases moving to VDI doesn't really affect the security of your desktops one way or the other.

Actually some people have argued that VDI can be *less* secure than traditional PCs and laptops, since in traditional environments attackers have to physically steal a laptop or physically break into your office building. With VDI, they just need to guess a user's password and they're in—from anywhere, from any device :), with full access!

Anyway, that's more of a discussion about VDI versus traditional PCs and laptops, but we're talking about DaaS in this book. Since DaaS is just VDI that's hosted somewhere else, what does that mean for security? How does hosting your desktops yourself compare with letting someone else host them?

A lot of it really comes down to how much you trust your provider!

For most enterprises, the single reason they choose *not* to go to DaaS is because they trust their own environment a lot more than they trust someone else's. So for them, secure VDI is on-premises VDI.

Ironically it might be the opposite for smaller and medium-sized companies. If your company of thirty people rents an office suite in a corporate office park that's abandoned at night and on weekends, it would be pretty easy for someone to break in a window or kick down a door to clean out everything in your office, including your servers. We would think that for those kinds of companies, moving the desktops to a "real" DaaS provider is *much* more secure than hosting them themselves.

Really you need to take an honest look at how secure the servers in your own office are—whether you use VDI or not. People are quick to say, "I don't trust the cloud," when in reality cloud providers are much more secure than many on-premises alternatives.

As a quick side story, we talked with a large company with a branch office of about fifty users. They said they "didn't trust the cloud," and because of that they had a server room at the branch office with a domain controller, a file server, an Exchange server, and so on. Their thinking was that this office was secure because it was on the fifth floor of a building with 24-hour guards and key-cards for entry. But the reality is that the guards just smile and wave on through anyone who doesn't look homeless, and the FedEx, UPS, USPS, Costco, fire marshal, building maintenance, and about another dozen people from different companies all have keycards. Heck, when we visited this company we just rang the doorbell and were let in! Who are we? How do they know we're not going to walk to their server room, kick through the door (it's an internal office door—it wouldn't stand a chance), grab the hard drives (they're hot-swap) and walk out! And they think *that's* more secure than the cloud? Think again!

On the other hand, you have to keep in mind that there's more than one kind of security. There's the objective technical security, and there's the psychological or emotional security of fully controlling your environment.

To understand the difference, imagine you run a small company where your website is critical. You could either have a web server in your office or use a hosted web service platform. Most everyone would objectively agree that a web hosting provider would have better security than what you could get with a server sitting in your office. No brainer, they win. But from the emotional side of things, it's comforting to know that *your* web server is in *your* office. You can see it and touch it. You know everything about it. You are comfortable with your level of backup and encryption and patching. Overall you just feel better about it.

Now compare that with a server hosted by someone else, where you may get physical anxiety over all the unknowns. Did a rogue employee just storm out? Is some other customer doing something illegal that will draw the attention of the feds? Are they paying their taxes on time? Are they still in business?

So when we talk about the security of a VDI or DaaS environment, it's important to separate out the technical security of the environment from the emotional security of knowing where everything is and how it works.

How VDI Deployment Options Affect Security

Let's step through how this would be applied to your various hosting options for VDI. From a high level, we could say you have three options (though in reality there are many variations of each of these):

- VDI that you build and host yourself inside your company.
- VDI that you build yourself but that you host in a colocation center.

- VDI that someone else builds and hosts for you (DaaS).

Each of these has several advantages and disadvantages when viewed through the lens of security. As we examine each of these, keep in mind that we're only going to look at the aspects of security that are different between each option. (In other words, yes, there are security issues around whether you use VDI or not, but that's not what we're looking at here, since these are all VDI options.)

The security of VDI hosted inside your company

The best part of hosting VDI inside your company is that it is just as secure as everything else you host inside your company. Sure, you could play all these games to try to figure out whether it's actually better or worse than a cloud provider or public data center. But really if you're hosting your own domain controllers, your file servers, your apps, your databases, and your email servers all in-house, your company is obviously comfortable with it. If you choose to host your VDI desktops on-premises as well, that's great. No problem!

The security of VDI you build and host in a public data center

This next option is for VDI that you design, build, and own yourself but host in a public data center that's shared with other companies. This is a nice hybrid approach because you get the security of a big building from a company that's dedicated to hosting. You get access to their fast internet pipes and backup power generators and everything, and you also get the security of knowing where your data is, knowing who has access to it, and knowing everything about your environment from the hardware up through the desktops.

Of course this method also means that you still need to have the *expertise* for everything from your hardware through your desktops. In this case you're the one who's responsible for swapping out failed hardware. You're the one who has to design the VDI, build it, and test it. When something breaks, unless it's the power or the internet connection, the responsibility falls on you to fix it. From a security standpoint this now means that you have to be an expert in server security and hypervisor security and VPNs and firewalls and encryption and everything else that you want to do in your environment.

The security of VDI someone else builds and hosts for you (DaaS)

The final VDI deployment option is for someone else to build, host, and maintain your VDI environment in their facilities. This is the true DaaS that we've been talking about in this book.

Unfortunately from a pure security standpoint, this is also the most risky. If your desktops are just up in the cloud somewhere, how do you know the facility is secure? Who has access to them? How are your desktops isolated from other customers' desktops? When a user logs in, how do you know he or she is booting up or connecting to one of your desktops? (You've heard of man-in-the-middle attacks? With DaaS, you could have an OS-in-the-middle attack!) How do you know that your disk image hasn't been compromised? How do you know that someone hasn't tampered with it or installed screen or key recording software?

Our feeling, unfortunately, is that without definitive answers to these questions, there's a big risk when it comes to the security and the unknowns of DaaS from the public cloud.

Making DaaS Secure

There's a joke (that we just made up) that goes like this: How do you create the most secure DaaS possible? Build the most secure desktop computing environment you can and then you call that "DaaS."

The joke works because the term "DaaS" means different things to different people, so the "most secure DaaS" also varies depending on whom you're talking to. Some people believe that traditional on-premises VDI is the same thing as in-house DaaS, and so in those cases traditional desktop and VDI security approaches would make that DaaS secure.

Others believe that the term "DaaS" can be used only when you're getting desktops from the public cloud, and still others believe that the public cloud can never be secure. So for those people, the answer to the question "How do you make DaaS secure?" is, "Don't use DaaS."

We know that it sounds like a cop-out, but we can't emphasize this enough. The real response to the question "Is DaaS secure?" or "How do you make DaaS secure?" is this: Who's asking? What do you mean by "DaaS?" And what do you mean by "make secure?" For your particular company, does making something secure mean certain standards and certifications have to be met? Does it mean you don't want data to get stolen? If so, are you trying to defend against employees or outside attackers?

Seriously, this is why there are entire books written about security. It's not as simple as your boss saying to you, "Hey, when we go to DaaS, make sure it's secure!"

Like all security, VDI and DaaS security is a balance between security, convenience, and cost. You can have two out of the three. You want secure and convenient? It's not going to be cheap. You want secure and cheap? It's not going to be convenient. You want convenient and cheap? It's not going to be secure.

When trying to secure your DaaS environment, the first thing to do is define your goals. What are you trying to secure exactly? Are you worried about employee IP theft? Competitors stealing your stuff? Government or industry regulations you have to comply with?

Second, even though we're talking about VDI and DaaS, remember that the vast majority of desktop security issues have to do with the Windows desktop OS (malware, antivirus, phishing, social engineering, and so on), so those still apply whether you're using desktop PCs, laptops, in-house VDI, or DaaS.

Taking all that into consideration, when you're thinking about the security of your actual DaaS environment, keep the following in mind:

- Security comes down to trust. How much do you trust your DaaS provider? Why? Is your trust based on actual facts or just a gut feeling?

- Ask your DaaS provider how they handle security. Do they offer drive or disk image encryption? If so, who has the keys?

- What are your authentication options? What about two-factor authentication?

- How does the DaaS provider validate you (the customer)? If you lose your password, how do you get it reset? If it's as simple as you calling in and resetting your account with security questions, what's to stop an attacker from Facebook stalking you and then calling the DaaS provider to reset "your" credentials? (This is a serious problem that many cloud providers do not adequately address.)

- How does your DaaS provider isolate their customers from each other? Are you each on separate hardware? Or just separate VMs on the same hardware? Or just separate sessions on the same VM? Does this matter to you?

- What about storage? Do you share storage with your competitors? If the FBI raids the DaaS provider because someone else is doing bad things, will they take the servers and storage that you're using too?

- Are you on the same network as other customers? How is the isolation of networks done? Does the DaaS provider's management network cross over into your DaaS environment, or are they separate?

- Are you able to run audits on the people who accessed your environment? Are you able to audit who from the DaaS provider accessed your environment and see what they did?

Again, the thing to keep in mind with security is that DaaS is Windows desktops running on a VDI platform hosted in the cloud. So to do security right, you need to read books on Windows desktop security, VDI security, and cloud security. Unfortunately that will probably amount to 2,000 pages of reading and by the time you're done, you'll just want to curl up into a ball on the floor and cry. All we can say is good luck with that.

The good news is that DaaS providers are accustomed to answering questions like these. People we talked to didn't so much as pause to think about their answers. As long as you know what to ask, you can find out the answers you need to determine if the level of security is enough for you.

The Bottom Line for DaaS Security

Look, we can beat around the bush all day, but let's just come out and say it: Based on conversations we had when researching this book, if you're a big enterprise company who's worried about security, you're not going to do DaaS. Period. Conversation over. There are just too many unknowns, especially as we mentioned already with the whole, "we don't know what we don't know," fear. If those types of customers want the benefits of VDI, they're going to build and host it themselves.

But for small and medium-sized companies, or companies that aren't in regulated environments, DaaS sure is an easy way to get up and running on VDI, and trustworthy DaaS providers are almost certainly more capable of delivering a secure VDI environment than what these customers can do on their own.

14. Client Devices and BYOD

One of the great things about VDI (and, by extension, DaaS) is that it separates the execution of the Windows desktop environment from the device the user uses to access that desktop. While this seems awesome at first, you quickly realize, "Wait, so this means now my users can access Windows from *anything*? Whoa... I'm gonna need a minute."

It's pretty much true though. When you move to VDI or DaaS, your users can access their Windows desktops from traditional desktop PCs, laptops, Macs, tablets, phones, thin clients, Kindle Fires, Xboxes, smart TVs, that new Samsung refrigerator that runs Android (seriously, that's a thing), and about a thousand other devices—pretty much anything with a screen that connects to the internet.

So what does this mean for you as an administrator? Does DaaS mean that you *don't* have to be involved in the decision around client devices? Or does it mean that you *do* have to be involved, since there are now so many choices? And whose call is it really? Yours? What about the DaaS provider? Do they have specific requirements or recommendations?

How to Pick the 'Right' Client Device

We put the word "right" in quotes because like many things in life, there's no truly right or wrong client device for DaaS. But since there are so many options, there are certainly certain types of devices that make more sense in some situations over others, so that's what we're trying to think through here.

Regardless of whether you, your users, or your DaaS provider will pick the client devices, there are a few questions you need to answer to figure out which types will be a good fit:

- Is your DaaS replacing your users' desktops or augmenting them?
- How mobile are your users?
- What are your users' usage patterns?

Will your DaaS desktops replace or augment other desktops?

The biggest thing that will affect your client choice relates to how your users will use their DaaS desktops. Is it your goal for the DaaS desktop to totally replace your users' local desktops? Or are you just using DaaS for certain applications while your users access other apps outside of DaaS? (SaaS web applications are a good example of this. If you have a DaaS desktop and your users also need to use Salesforce, do you intend for them to access Salesforce from the browser on their DaaS desktop, or will they access it from a local browser on their client device outside of the DaaS environment?)

Obviously if your intention is that the DaaS desktops will be used for everything, you want a client that's purpose-built for DaaS and doesn't require much management locally. (Just reusing your existing desktop PCs in this case might not be ideal, since you'd still have to manage, patch, and maintain them, and for what? Just to access the DaaS desktop? It's kind of a waste of effort.)

On the other hand, if you're providing DaaS for some applications while relying on a local client to do others, obviously you'll need to choose a device based on its ability to meet the local computing needs of your users. (It has to have the browser they need, etc.)

How mobile are your users?

"Supporting mobility" is one of the rallying cries of people who love VDI and DaaS. But what exactly does "mobility" mean? There are actually two very different ways this word is used, and you need to figure out which one you're thinking about when you say you want to support mobility.

One way refers to the mobile devices themselves. Even though laptops are lightweight and portable nowadays, most people think of touch-based devices like phones and tablets when they think of mobile devices. Obviously DaaS clients exist for all mobile device platforms, so it is certainly an option to extend your enterprise applications to them. (Though accessing desktop applications from touch-based devices doesn't provide the best user experience, at least it's possible.)

The other way describes the users, not the devices. The mobile user is someone who's constantly on the go, working from home, then the office, then the hotel, then the coffee shop, then the office, then home, etc. While mobile users might choose mobile devices for quick tasks while they're on the bus, the bulk of this type of mobile user's time is still spent sitting down in front of more traditional computing setups, including one or more large displays, a keyboard, and a mouse.

What are your users' usage patterns?

How your users will use their DaaS desktops affects the client choice as much as the applications they use. For example, if a user stays in the DaaS desktop all day, every day, that's a very different usage pattern than with someone who's constantly jumping in and out and switching between remote and local apps five times an hour.

DaaS Client Options

Even though there are so many different client options out there, we'd like to go through some of the things you should know about the most popular types of clients, including:

- Thin clients
- Desktop PCs
- Laptops
- iPads and mobile phones

Throughout all this remember that client choice is not an all-or-nothing decision. You might have most of your users on one type of client with others sprinkled in here and there as you need them. Also keep in mind that the whole point of VDI and DaaS is to separate the Windows desktop from the client device, so even if you assign one user to a thin client, there's no reason that user shouldn't also be able to access the DaaS desktop from his or her phone, iPad, or home computer as needed.

Thin clients

We assume you've heard of thin clients before. They're like small, cheap desktop PCs without the guts. They have all the standard connectors—display, USB, audio, power, etc.—except they can't do anything apart from connecting to a remote VDI or DaaS desktop. One of the users we talked with described her thin client as a "cable box for her Windows desktop."

Thin clients are great for DaaS environments where the DaaS desktop replaces a local desktop PC. They're perfect for users who sit at a desk all day, since they support the keyboards, mice, displays, and peripherals that users need, and they're much simpler to manage than full desktop PCs because they don't run anything locally other than the bare minimum tools they need to connect to the remote DaaS desktop.

You may already have thin clients in your company to access an existing VDI or RDSH environment. If you do, and you don't want to replace them, you'll need to account for whatever remoting protocols they support when choosing a DaaS provider. For example, if you have an office full of Teradici chip-based zero clients, you're pretty much locked into a DaaS provider who uses PC-over-IP, such as VMware Desktone or AWS WorkSpaces.)

On the other hand, if you decide you want to buy new thin clients to replace your desktop PCs, you have a lot of options. You have your choice of operating system, such as custom Linux builds, embedded versions of Windows, and Android. You also have your choice of a range of capabilities, including how much graphical content they can support and how many displays you can connect. And of course you have a wide range of price points, starting around $100 and going up to well over $500.

There are millions of words of argument on the internet about the merits of thin clients versus PCs. (In fact, we authors are responsible for a healthy portion of them—sorry!) The bigger issue behind those arguments is not whether a thin client is better than a PC but rather whether you're ready to move from Windows running on the client device (the old way) to Windows running in a data center (the VDI/DaaS way).

But since this is a book about DaaS and we're in a section focused on client devices, we're going to assume that you've already made the decision to go to VDI or DaaS for at least some of your users, so we can now focus on thin clients versus desktop PCs instead of VDI Windows versus local Windows.

Desktop PCs

One of the benefits that DaaS providers tout is reuse of your existing desktop PCs, or, they'll say, "DaaS is cheaper because you can extend the life of your desktop PCs." What they're really saying is you'll essentially turn your existing desktop PC into a thin client. The idea is that even though the oldest desktops in your environment are getting kind of slow, they're still fast enough to run the DaaS connection client and perfectly capable to connect your users to their remote DaaS desktops.

Doing this conversion can be as simple as telling the user, "Hey, when you turn on your computer tomorrow, just go to mydaasprovider.com from now on and don't use any of the locally installed programs." Or you could reformat the user's desktop, choosing to install only the bare minimum software. There are actually two approaches to this.

The first is to use a solution from just about any of the thin client vendors to replace Windows on a PC with an OS that is specifically made to be a thin client. (Each vendor has their own.) This approach has two benefits. First is that you can manage both your desktop PCs and thin clients from the same management interface. Second is that when a PC finally breaks down you can simply replace it with a thin client without having to change anything on your back-end. Also, if you use a solution like this, you no longer have to manage Windows on the desktop PCs, so you don't have to worry about updates and lockdowns and stuff.

The other approach you can take to reuse your PCs is to use a thin client conversion or kiosk solution like Norskale Thin Client Transformer, ThinKiosk, or ThinLaunch Thin Desktop, among others. You can use these to lock down a Windows desktop PC, essentially turning it into a thin client. Keep in mind, though, that these are still leveraging Windows, so they'll need to be locked down hard and updated regularly. You're still managing Windows, after all.

Using your existing hardware with Windows is convenient, and generally speaking we like the solution. Everything works and fits together. (No surprises like, "Hey, these new thin clients only have HDMI outputs and my monitors only have VGA inputs, so now I have to buy a new monitor for every user.") And we also generally find that the Windows versions of the DaaS clients tend to be the most fully featured, so if you can throw Windows 7 on your four-year-old desktop PCs and get another five years of use out of them as DaaS thin clients, that sounds good to us!

Our only crucial piece of advice is to suggest that if you do repurpose your existing PCs into thin clients, do something (anything!) to make sure you've locked them down and are centrally managing them. Remember that Windows acting like a thin client is still Windows, so if you just wipe out all your old Windows XP machines and install Windows 7, you are *technically* still going to have to manage them all. And that's in addition to all the DaaS desktops that you're managing. So in this case, you're kind of managing *two* desktops for every user. (D'oh!)

The good news is that since the newly converted thin client PCs really only need the DaaS client installed (and maybe a browser), they should be much simpler to manage than full, persistent Windows images. If you can just lock them down and centrally push out updates, you should be all set. (Whether you choose one of the prepacked thin client conversions or go at it on your own, just please do something!)

And don't forget, you can easily swap any PCs-turned-thin-client with "real" thin clients as they break. Just buy a few new thin clients and keep them in the closet, and as the older desktops die, even a novice user ought to be able to match up all the connector shapes to get the new thin client up and running.

Laptops

There's a lot of debate about whether VDI (and therefore DaaS) is an appropriate technology for laptop users. On the "yes" side of the argument people say, "Hey, 3G, 4G, and WiFi networks are becoming ubiquitous, and if you want the benefits of VDI, why wouldn't you want to extend those benefits to your laptop users too?"

The flip side of that is that the whole point of laptops is because people are mobile, and there are plenty of situations where internet connectivity is not available or is so slow or inconsistent that using DaaS would be an awful experience.

Our view, like that on almost everything, is that whether a laptop makes a good DaaS client depends on what you're using DaaS for.

If you're *replacing* your users' desktop environments with DaaS, that means your users can't do any work without their DaaS desktop. In those cases we believe it's probably not a good idea to make laptop users use DaaS.

But if you're using DaaS only for a few Windows applications here and there—maybe just for one project workspace or a few line-of-business applications—it's probably okay for laptop users to do most of their work locally on their laptop but to also use the DaaS environment for the few specific things they need.

Laptops are also fine for BYO-type scenarios (which we'll discuss more below). We like the idea of saying, "Hey, we're using DaaS for your work desktop. We're putting a thin client on your desk at work, and you can access the DaaS desktop from your home computer or your iPad if you want." In that case, if a user has his or her own laptop to access the DaaS environment, that seems fine to us. In fact, using a laptop for BYO is almost preferred because it means users can do their personal things (Facebook, games, etc.) on their laptop instead of mucking up their DaaS desktop with all of that.

IPads and mobile phones

So many companies selling DaaS talk about how it's a great solution for your iPad users. They talk about how their DaaS platform lets you convert your Windows desktop apps to iPad apps.

There's only one thing you need to know about connecting to a Windows desktop running on VDI or DaaS from an iPad: It sucks. This is not VDI's fault or DaaS's fault but rather because Windows desktop applications were designed to be used on big screens with keyboards and mice. The iPad (or any tablet or phone really) has a single small screen and no keyboard, which means when you need to type something, the virtual, on-screen, "soft" keyboard consumes even more of your already limited screen real estate. When clicking with the mouse, tablet users have to tap it with their finger. While that's an intuitive concept, people's fingertips are not nearly as precise as mouse pointers, so they end up having to play this constant game of zoom-zoom-zoom-tap-pan-pan-pan-tap-zoom-zoom-zoom. It's like entering the Konami Code over and over again.

That said, VDI technology makers like Citrix and VMware try to help out iPad users as much as possible. While today's VDI clients (which are the DaaS clients too) for the iPad have different tools and ways of working with the keyboard to try to smooth out the rough edges, they don't get around the fundamental issue that

Windows desktop applications were not designed to be used from devices like iPads.

So from our standpoint, while a VDI or DaaS desktop should not be someone's primary computing environment on an iPad, it can be convenient for critical business applications that are needed on the go. (You wouldn't force users to do all their work from the iPad via VDI or DaaS. Rather, you'd have them run their email and browser and document viewers as normal iPad apps and use the DaaS connection only for the apps that don't have web or iPad alternatives.)

There's a huge opportunity here, if any clever readers want to take it on, to provide some type of application "transformation" wrapper that would convert traditional Windows desktop applications to be more touch-friendly. We envision this would work as a Windows desktop application that acts as a sort of proxy UI to the actual application. You'd still use VDI and the normal remoting protocols to deliver this touch-friendly UI to your users, since the back-end desktop application still has to run on Windows. But the idea is that this wrapper UI would look and feel more appropriate on touch-based devices with small screens.

Because we suspect that this proxy application wouldn't be able to configure itself, some admin somewhere would have to "design" the new UI for each Windows desktop app. After all, if the desktop version of the application has a million tiny buttons and menu items, you'd need some human input to decide what's most important to expose to the user on a small screen.

Citrix offers something similar with their Mobile SDK for Windows Apps, but this is limited to applications where you can access the source code, since you have to tie it into the SDK. It works well, and Citrix can possibly make it better if they choose to use some of the technology they recently acquired from Framehawk, but there is still room in the industry for a general-purpose app-refactoring solution (if it's even possible).

Maybe someone does this already? If so, we haven't found it. But if an offering like this did come out, it would be pretty great because you could use DaaS to host legacy Windows applications that would work well (or as well as they could) on phones and tablets.

Using DaaS to Solve BYO

One of the hot trends in IT today is BYOC (bring your own computer) or BYOD (bring your own device), often simply shortened to BYO. Most of the companies selling DaaS claim that "enabling BYO" or "solving BYO" is one of the benefits of DaaS. So is it?

Again, that depends. It's true that one of the great advantages of VDI and DaaS technology is that there are client software agents for just about every platform in the world. Windows, Mac OS, Linux, Windows Phone, BlackBerry, iOS, Android... there's client software to connect to VDI from all of them. Heck, many VDI and DaaS providers even have full HTML5-based clients, meaning you can connect to a remote desktop simply by visiting a website, with no client installation or download needed!

So in that case, yes, DaaS does "solve" BYO because it lets your users bring in and connect to your desktop from whatever device they want. Score one for BYO. DaaS doesn't solve every BYO challenge though. For example, some users might choose MacBooks because, you know, *they want to use a Mac!* The problem is that your DaaS environment is Windows. So yes, *technically* the user can bring in a Mac, and yes, *technically* the DaaS software will work perfectly, but the result is that the user's nice Mac OS X desktop will be completely covered up by the Windows DaaS desktop you're delivering. Is that Mac-loving user going to be happy? ("Yay! I'm using a Mac at work!") Or upset? ("WTF? Where did my Mac go, and why does this look like Windows?")

The other gotcha around BYO is with iPads, as we mentioned in the previous section. A lot of people think, "Hey, now that I have DaaS my users can use any device they choose!" Users think, "Awesome, the device I choose is an iPad." So yes, the iPad will *technically* work and connect fine to the DaaS desktop, but it might be annoying to use. (Though this really depends on the user and how much pain tolerance he or she has in relation to wanting to convey the right social image. We've seen people use iPads to connect to DaaS desktops with little battery-powered keyboard cases and MiFi adapters and all sorts of things, and we're like, "Dude, why not just replace your Rube Goldberg contraption with a cheap laptop?" Typically they give us a funny look and say, "But I'm using an *iPad!*")

So can DaaS enable BYO? Yeah, definitely. Using DaaS means that your users can use whatever devices they want, and apart from helping them get the client software installed, you don't have to be in the business of managing or maintaining their devices. A remote Windows desktop might not be the ideal solution for all users, but at least they can access it from whatever device they want.

Picking the Right Client Device for DaaS

So given all this, how do you pick the devices your users should use? (Or how do you create a list of devices you'll support and devices that are ideal?) Here again is where you can lean on your DaaS provider. The first thing we'd ask the provider is which devices and platforms they recommend and what levels of support are offered for each.

Next is to be aware of the capabilities of any devices you buy. Remember that if you buy a device that supports only one remoting protocol, you're locked into that protocol for as long as you own that device and that would really limit your choice of DaaS providers if you ever want to switch in the future.

The ultimate decision as to what clients to choose for DaaS boils down to what devices your users want to use, how much you want to be involved in the decision, what applications they'll use locally and via DaaS, and how much time they'll spend in each environment. The good news is there are a lot of choices out there, and it's easy to mix and match as you need.

15. How to Pick a DaaS Solution

Wow! So far we've looked at VDI, we've talked about DaaS, and we've gone over all the things you have to figure out as you design your DaaS solution. Now we're *finally* to the point where we can help you make the decision that's essentially the whole point of this book. Now it's time to pick a DaaS solution. Hooray!

There's a lot that goes into this. Before you can even pick the provider, you have to figure out what you're looking for. After all, not all providers offer all options, so that's what we'll look at first, beginning with a look at the various DaaS platforms.

What Is a DaaS Platform?

"Wait," you might be thinking, "I thought the DaaS provider *was* the platform? So why are you saying we have to look at the DaaS platform?" It's a good question, because there is a key difference between platform and provider, which needs some explaining.

The DaaS platform is the back-end software that the DaaS provider builds their DaaS solution on. You can think of it as being kind of like the "DaaS OS" that the provider uses. Just like the hundreds of different television makers in the world buy their LCD display panels from one of four manufacturers, there are only a handful of DaaS platforms that power the hundreds of DaaS providers in the world. Let's look at a few of the most popular ones.

First is Desktone, which was purchased by VMware in 2013. VMware's Desktone platform powers the DaaS offerings from VMware (obviously), Dell, NaviSite (now owned by Time Warner Cable), Fujitsu, NEC, and many others.

Then there's Citrix. They don't have separate DaaS platform per se, rather, Citrix has created a Cloud Service Provider (CSP) license that DaaS providers can use to build hosted XenApp and XenDesktop solutions. Many of them are actually built on servers in the Amazon Web Services EC2 cloud. (Note that this is not the same as AWS WorkSpaces.) Citrix currently has over 2,000 service providers signed up for the CSP program, although not all of them are delivering desktops or applications. Citrix is also continuing to build more multi-tenancy and orchestration features into XenDesktop specifically for DaaS use cases.

Nimdesk and dinCloud also have platforms in this space that are available to other providers to license. DinCloud, for example, licenses their desktops through a channel much like any other application, so even your local VAR could hook you up with dinCloud desktops.

Microsoft is also circling around DaaS, and while they haven't officially announced anything as we're writing this, it's widely expected that they'll build some kind of service on Azure that will deliver either Windows desktops or Windows applications as a service. (The current rumor is that this is called Project Mohoro, so you can google that if you want to learn more.)

Then there's Amazon Web Services (AWS), which recently announced their WorkSpaces DaaS offering. (Actually we can credit AWS's entry into this space for giving us the final push to write this book. We had been kicking around the idea for the past year or so, but AWS's entry meant that suddenly everyone was talking and asking us about DaaS, and we felt that lots of people needed some, um, education. So thanks, Jeff!)

Even though AWS WorkSpaces appears more like a fully packaged direct-to-consumer DaaS solution, we believe it will ultimately have a larger impact on the world in the form of infrastructure that powers other DaaS providers' offerings. After all, most of AWS's other offerings are back-end plays. Take S3, for example. When S3 was first announced, it was possible for consumers to download S3 clients to use the storage themselves. But the concept of internet-based file storage didn't really take off until Dropbox released their product. And do you know what the back-end storage for Dropbox was? Amazon S3!

We envision the same thing happening for AWS WorkSpaces. Sure, some consumers and enterprises will use it directly, but we ultimately see WorkSpaces becoming a cloud-based DaaS platform that other DaaS providers use to sell their own offerings.

Picking a DaaS Platform

Okay, so now we've established that all these different platforms exist. So what? Should you really care about the back-end differences? Again, isn't that the whole reason you're going with DaaS?

We recommend that when you're evaluating DaaS providers, you ask them about their platform. See how much they're willing to tell you or how secretive they are. Some DaaS providers regard their platform as a sort of trade secret, feeling that divulging the details about it will lead to IP theft or something. Hey, if your name is Amazon Web Services, we'll accept that as an answer. You've obviously proved that you know what you're doing. But if you're Bob's Discount House of DaaS, a wink and a promise that we can relax and trust you isn't going to cut it. We're going to need you to divulge a bit more.

Some people say, "But hey, who cares? Just make sure your service-level agreement covers what you need. Then it doesn't matter whether the platform is good, since you're covered if not." We'll discuss SLAs in depth in the next section, but the short answer here is that you have to trust your DaaS provider enough to believe they can actually fulfill the terms of their SLA. It's the whole "talk is cheap" thing, and no amount of legal-sounding mumbo jumbo is going to make you feel better when your desktops are down.

So talk to your DaaS provider about their platform to make sure you have a comfortable feeling about it. Ask them about how they handle multi-tenancy, for instance, to make sure (A) they know what multi-tenancy is, and (B) they have a plan to keep your company's desktops separate from other customers' (which could even be your competitors).

Actually, wait . . . do *you* know what multi-tenancy is? In the context of DaaS, multi-tenancy means a provider (like your DaaS provider) has multiple customers (or "tenants") on the same hardware and platform. Saying that a system supports multi-tenancy just means that it's designed to make sure that one customer's stuff is isolated and doesn't get mixed up with someone else's. You wouldn't want to open Windows Explorer on your DaaS desktop and find out that the c:\temp folder you're seeing is shared by other users from other customers at the same time!

Also ask your DaaS provider about how they handle security, how they make sure that nobody is accidentally provisioned with the wrong customer's desktops, and how they isolate your networking and storage from other customers'. Based on the provider's answers, you'll be able to decide if the level of security and isolation fits with your needs. The more transparent a company is in response to your questions, the better. (In general we found that the DaaS providers were very open and willing to share details about their platforms. Then again, we were writing a book about it, so they had every reason to be nice to us!)

While we're on the subject of how you can get comfortable with a potential DaaS provider, you should also ask for reference customers that you can speak with. Ask around social networks and at conferences too. See if the provider has a good reputation or a shady one (some are better than others, for sure).

Platform lock-in

Another thing to keep in mind when choosing a DaaS platform is that you're basically locked into whichever one you choose. The back-end hypervisors, virtual machines, automation, and even the protocols are specific to each platform, so once you choose, you're pretty much stuck with that.

However, that does not mean that you're locked into the actual DaaS provider. In fact, since so many providers share the same platform, you can actually use that to your advantage to get added flexibility. For instance, you could spread your DaaS load across multiple providers so you don't have to put all your eggs in one basket, or to address any geographical concerns. If you have offices in Japan, San Francisco, and New York, and you can find providers in each of those places that share, for instance, the Citrix platform, you can direct clients to the most appropriate provider. If you choose to store your data with the provider too, this can help address the issue of data sovereignty by keeping one country's data inside that country.

The other thing that using multiple providers can do is provide a hedge against one going out of business. For instance, if you have your desktops spread across two Desktone providers and one of them disappears, your users can automatically (or with very little effort) connect to the other provider and receive the same experience. If, for some reason, the second provider doesn't have the capacity (because it's doing the same thing for every other customer of the company that went belly up), you can spread the load around to many providers.

So platform lock-in doesn't have to be a negative thing. Maybe we should call it platform commitment? (Wait, now we sound like Microsoft licensing folks!) Regardless, "committing" to a particular DaaS platform opens you up to a network of providers that leverage it. You can potentially end up with a more flexible solution, which ultimately makes it a more resilient and trustworthy solution.

DaaS Versus IaaS Versus PaaS

If you've been paying attention to the cloud space over the past few years, you're undoubtedly familiar with the terms Infrastructure as a Service (IaaS) and Platform as a Service (PaaS), which at first blush sound like DaaS. We agree.

We perceive IaaS to be more like an umbrella term that describes getting all different types of IT infrastructure as a service (virtual machines, storage, VLANs, and so on), while PaaS is one level above that (Windows servers, web servers, and databases). So in our view, DaaS is simply one of many PaaS offerings. Of course we're not the authority on the official -aaS naming conventions, and people may view DaaS, IaaS, and PaaS differently, but that's how we see the relationship.

So DaaS is built on top of IaaS. IaaS handles the multi-tenancy, security, and isolation, and DaaS adds the desktops, the connection brokering, the provisioning, and so on. It gets interesting when you look at the components of your own environment that you've outsourced to an IaaS provider, because if the provider also offers DaaS, you might just be able to go with that and be done with it. After all, you trust your provider with other important aspects of your business, so it's not too far of a leap to trust them with your desktops. They already have infrastructure services specific to your company configured, and you already know how to work with one another.

But what if you've outsourced some infrastructure to an IaaS provider that isn't offering DaaS? Do you wait for them to get on board so that your life is easier, or do you look elsewhere? If you decide to look elsewhere, do you move your infrastructure to that company as well? After all, there's no point in having it split really. And if you'd do it to hedge your bets on downtime, ask yourself what good one is without the other? Also, by having two providers, you're actually doubling your chance of a single failure.

So it would seem that you need to decide how badly you want to do DaaS. Do you want to do it badly enough that you'll move your infrastructure to a company that also does desktops, or will you wait for your IaaS provider to add DaaS to their list? If you can't wait, will you move your IaaS to another provider that also offers DaaS, or will you build your own VDI environment at the IaaS provider? Either one of these is a big project.

Understanding DaaS Service-Level Agreements

Another topic that comes up when shopping around for DaaS providers is the ubiquitous service-level agreement (SLA), which describes what level of service your provider guarantees and how they will compensate you should they fail to deliver on what they agreed to.

Thinking about SLAs with desktops is interesting, because they never really existed before outside of some kind of company IT policy document. (Our desktop SLA is, "If you break your desktop, we will fix it within two weeks" or whatever.) Even with VDI, the SLA is pretty much on you. If all the desktops are down, you're just trying to get them back up as fast as you can. At that point you're not really thinking about what your IT policy is.

But when it comes to DaaS, if your desktops are down, you're at the mercy of the provider. How fast will they fix them? The answer depends on (A) their *ability* to fix them, and (B) your SLA, which dictates how quickly they're required to fix them.

Actually those are the two things you need to remember when you're talking about SLAs with your DaaS provider.

First, keep in mind that your SLA can say whatever it wants, but when things are going badly, the SLA is just words on paper. Your DaaS provider might promise no more than 10 minutes of downtime per month. That's great. But do they have the technical competence to back that up? And if so, how would you know (or not know) before you signed that contract?

The other aspect of an SLA is that it describes how you will be compensated if the provider fails to meet it. What if your DaaS provider is down for half a day, leaving you with no desktops and a loss of hundreds of thousands of dollars? That would not be the time you'd want to find that the DaaS provider can say, "Okay, you are paying us $50 per month, per desktop, and 24 × 31 = 744 hours in the month. You were down for four hours, so that's 4 ÷ 744 = 0.0053% of the time, so go ahead and deduct 26 cents off of next month's invoice!"

Keep in mind that SLAs don't have to be black-or-white up-or-down. You might have an SLA that describes how fast your desktops run, guaranteeing you a certain connection time or number of storage IOPS. This is another area where everyone is different, so you'll just have to talk to your DaaS provider and see what they offer. And remember, everything is negotiable!

Choosing a DaaS Provider

Now we're into the meat of the discussion. How do you choose the DaaS provider that's the most appropriate one for you? Sadly, this isn't one of those situations where we can list out all the pros and cons of each one, so don't expect that. This market is young and changes fast, so any specific thing we write will be obsolete by the time you read it. Plus, there are hundreds, if not thousands, of DaaS providers that are built on the half-dozen or so platforms, so comparing them would be a monumental task. (But if you want to start daaslist.com, we'll tweet you!) Keep in mind, too, that everything is negotiable, so if you can't find the perfect solution for your needs, you can probably put together what you want by talking through your options with a few different providers.

So what does it actually take to pick a provider? We believe you need to examine the following two things:

- Trust
- Flexibility

Picking a provider to trust

We explored the issue of trust earlier, and we left off by suggesting that if you're going to judge the trustworthiness of the DaaS provider and its employees, you should do the same with your own employees. It's foolish to think that your employees are any more trustworthy than your provider's, unless of course you're in some high-security environment where everyone has a dossier and clearance. (Though based on recent leaks in the United States, we're not sure if we can even take it that far.)

Getting past trust issues is paramount when considering the move to DaaS. If you've already outsourced other components of your infrastructure like email, web apps, or databases, you're less inclined to be hung up on trust. You'd also be in the minority, so congratulations, fellow thought leader! It's a fun club to be in (until you're proven wrong).

So how do you get past the trust issues? There are independent certifications that can help increase the level of trust for just about any organization. We're not going to pretend to be security experts (since an actual security expert wouldn't believe us anyway), but we can tell you that if you require a certain level of security, ask prospective DaaS providers if they have such certifications. You'll know better than we do about what exactly you need to feel comfortable.

Also keep in mind the lesson from before, which is a thief is a thief. If someone wants your data, he or she will get it. Like the velociraptors in *Jurassic Park*, they'll poke around until they find a weak spot and then exploit it. DaaS changes none of that.

Still, we're only talking about security-related trust. There are other ways in which you have to trust your DaaS provider. Do they know what they're doing? Will they stay in business?

Trust that your DaaS provider knows how to run your desktops

Straight from the "nobody does it better than we can do it" department, this trust issue is probably the most common concern we hear. Many organizations believe that they can do their own VDI better because it's *their* desktops, for *their* users, running in *their* office, completely managed by *their* IT department. Those organizations are misinformed. Actually that's being too nice—those organizations are just plain wrong.

Look, we're talking about a pissing contest between someone at a bar (that's you) and "Firehose" Phil, Jerk Face World Champion since 2007. Yeah, you can hold your own—especially after you've had a few—but Firehose Phil has turned this into a career! You (or someone you know—we're not picking on you specifically) may do a ton of research on VDI, go to conferences, take some training, and come back to the office swarley enough to think that you can pull off the greatest VDI project ever. But at the end of the day these DaaS providers don't have to worry about other distractions. They are 100% focused on delivering desktops. Every employee, every server, every SAN, every switch, and every router was set up for the sole purpose of delivering DaaS desktops. You. Cannot. Do. Better. Than. That.

We use email to illustrate this point. Companies that are reluctant to move their email to Gmail often cite something about downtime, like, "What if Gmail goes down and we don't have access to our email and calendars?" And they quickly add, "We don't have an SLA with them, so how do we know we're going to get good service?"

Our answer to them is that if Gmail goes down, it's worldwide news. It's an embarrassment to Google. You don't *need* an SLA because if Gmail goes down, there will be 425 million other people all pissed off at Google.

Now let's say Gmail goes down. Almost half a billion people are mad as hell, including your boss, because that one IT person (you?) insisted Gmail would be fine. So what do you do in that situation? You do nothing. You just sit there like everyone else, knowing that Google has a couple of hundred super-nerds who *literally wrote Gmail* trying to fix the problem. That's awesome.

What if you decided to run your own on-premises Exchange Server instead? When that goes down, what do you do? Google has 200 world-class engineers looking into their outage. And you? You have Ray, your Exchange-certified admin, and you've paged him twice. No offense to Ray, but who has a better chance of fixing their email first? Google? Or Ray?

When it comes to apples-to-apples comparisons, you simply cannot compete with the quality of service delivered by a company whose sole existence is to deliver that product. The only way that argument starts to break down is when you want to add flexibility or certain features that the provider can't offer, but at that point you're not talking apples-to-apples. It's not about being able to build a better VDI but about choosing the right solution for the use cases you have. Not everything is a good fit for VDI or DaaS, but if you have a use case that could be addressed by both technologies, the DaaS solution will be the better one.

Trust that the company will always be around

The other trust-based issue that comes up frequently is one that is exceptionally hard to gauge. Do you trust that the DaaS provider you choose will still be in business in the future? Actually the question is more like, "Will your DaaS provider still be in business when you decide you no longer want to do DaaS, or will they be the *reason* you no longer do DaaS?"

It's the stuff nightmares are made of. You wake up one morning to find 36 missed calls on your phone. The voicemails and texts are troubling because every single one of them says "I can't log into my desktop!" (Okay, we're being dramatic, since real users don't talk like that. They'll say something more like, "I turned on my work TV but I don't see my grandkids on my screen saver.") After you arrive at the office, you realize that the company that hosts your desktops isn't just offline—they're out of business.

Since DaaS is so new, there's bound to be several fly-by-night providers in the market that deliver solutions that are marginal at best. (Actually that's not necessarily fair. A lot of them have the best intentions in mind, but starting a company is hard. A lot of them will fail honorably.)

In the rush to get their products out the door, it's possible a DaaS provider's back-end is incomplete or not designed properly for highly available, high-performing, secure, isolated desktops. In addition to asking about the back-end platform, you might want to ask for the financial data from unknown providers.

While you're at it, compare their pricing with that of other providers. If the price is too good to be true, you should make a timely exit and start your search again. (We saw this with OnLive, who offered Windows 7-based DaaS desktops for $5 per month in 2012. It turned out they were in violation of Microsoft's licensing agreements, and to make a long story short, they're no longer offering Windows 7 DaaS desktops today.)

Sure, we're all looking for a good value, but it's important to keep in mind that DaaS is *not* going to be cheaper than traditional desktops, so stacking the deck in your favor by finding the absolute cheapest solution is not the best tactic. Did you learn about your provider because it offered a 2-for-1 Groupon? If so, move on to another provider.

Unfortunately there's no way to totally remove the risk that your provider may go belly up. Such is the risk of the cloud. The only surefire way to deal with this sort of thing (short of doing it all in-house) is to accept the risk and have an exit strategy.

Having an exit strategy means that before you choose a provider, before you sign the papers, you work out how you'd reclaim ownership of your desktops if the provider disappeared or you decide that you'd like to not do business with them anymore. We'll talk about how to develop an exit strategy later. For now just know that exit strategies are an important thing, and having a solid one can assuage some of your nervousness about your DaaS provider. (Think of an exit strategy as a prenup for DaaS.)

How flexible is your DaaS provider?

DaaS is about desktops. Desktops are used by users. Users are crazy. (Actually if you want to summarize this entire book in a tweet, that was it.) Even the best-laid plans for a one-size-fits-all desktop solution can be blown to smithereens by end-user activities.

We've talked about how DaaS providers—and cloud providers in general—strive to make their solutions as cookie-cutter as possible. That's how they offer the desktops so cheaply.

But what if you want more flexibility than that? This can manifest itself in two ways: You might want to be more "flexible" to do things differently from other customers, or you might want each desktop to be "flexible" in that it's more different than the others in your DaaS environment.

Some of these flexibility requests can be taken care of by paying your provider a few extra dollars on the front-end or as part of your monthly fee. Other requests might be possible only if you agree to do them yourself. And still others just might not be possible on the provider's platform, forcing you to rethink the importance of the request or to shop around for another provider. (Just keep in mind that the initial cost-per-desktop number you see is going to be for the cookie-cutter version.)

What kind of flexibility requests are we talking about here? It could be anything really. Maybe you want the DaaS provider to handle application patching, antivirus, and Windows updates? Maybe you want them to package all your applications and run an app store for you? Or maybe you need your DaaS connection broker to integrate with your custom-built on-premises user authentication system.

Summary

The most important thing we can leave you with when it comes to picking your DaaS platform and provider is that even though people talk about DaaS desktops as being in the cloud, you have to remember that the cloud is not a real thing. Your desktops aren't in "the cloud," they're in a data center somewhere, operated by your DaaS provider. If that data center or provider fails, you're in trouble.

So ask questions. Ask about the provider's data center. Ask about their backup plans. Ask about their insurance policies. Find out which data centers are closest to your users (since those ought to have the lowest latencies). Ask about security plans and multi-tenancy.

And most important, ask your provider to help you make a plan to leave them one day.

16. Migrating to DaaS

At this point we've talked about VDI and DaaS. You've designed your solution, picked your platform, and found a DaaS provider you trust. You're just about ready to do the actual migration.

Assessing Your Current Environment

One of the things we cannot stress enough is that you need to have a solid understanding of your current environment before migrating to DaaS, especially if your DaaS desktops will replace your existing physical desktops. As we mentioned at the beginning of this book when we talked about VDI, one of the biggest reasons VDI fails is that people underestimate (or don't know) what their users actually do in their desktops, and they're caught off guard once they move those desktops to VDI. The same can happen with DaaS.

Before you migrate to DaaS, you have to perform an assessment of your current desktop environment, including finding out what your users actually do all day, what applications they use, and how they use them. The good news is there are several software-based assessment tools that you can run on your existing physical desktop and laptop environment to help you get a better understanding of it. We mentioned a few already, like Lakeside Software SysTrack Virtual Machine Planner or Liquidware Labs Stratusphere. Products like these install agents on your physical desktops that monitor everything that happens, including network utilization, storage impact, what applications the users use, and even how graphically intensive those applications are. Then they create a report that shows you what you need to know about each user as you move toward your migration phase, including which users might be good candidates for shared non-persistent images and which might require persistent desktops.

Citrix also has a tool, AppDNA, that analyzes your existing Windows applications and lets you know whether they can be virtualized with popular app virtualization platforms. If you're moving to a Citrix-based DaaS platform, you might be able to get this tool for free.

Even if you don't use one of these automated tools, you need to make sure you have a solid understanding of your current desktop environment before you move ahead with your migration planning.

Defining the Scope

When doing your DaaS research, it's easy to get caught up in all the hype surrounding cloud technologies. There are some really exciting options with obvious benefits, like cloud storage or Infrastructure as a Service. It's easy to start thinking, "Wow, we could really use some of this too. Let's just go for it and move everything at the same time!"

This is a slippery slope. You just started with the idea that you want to move some desktops to the cloud, and then all of a sudden you're moving all your file servers and half of your data center up there too! Each one of these additional migration items tacks significant time onto you DaaS project and increases the risk that you will fail. So it's important that you make a solid decision about exactly what you're going to do and stick to it.

Of course we talked about how cloud-based file servers would make your DaaS migration easier, and that if that's something you're prepared to do, you should do that first. So if you decide that you want to do that migration, make sure everyone understands that it's a separate project from your DaaS migration. Whether you do it first or do them both at the same time, you want to keep the DaaS migration itself as clean as possible, as that's how you'll ensure the highest chance of success.

The bottom line is that everyone knows what scope creep is. It's one thing if you're just working on an internal IT project, but since DaaS involves external service providers with very specific contracts, timelines, and SLAs, you really have to be aware of what is and isn't involved in your project. And changes or additions need to be thought through in a purposeful way, not just, "Oh hey, can you do this too?"

Picking Your Users

Next up is picking the users that you'll convert over to DaaS. You have to think about both how many users you'll migrate and which users you'll migrate. Treat this as you would any major migration and deploy your new desktops and desktop images to a few people at a time early on. Then test, fix, and repeat.

When you pick your first batch of users—a.k.a. The Lucky Ones—find those who exemplify the use case that led you to DaaS in the first place. Also be sure to pick a wide range of tech-savviness, not just the power users or just the know-nothings. You need to make sure that what you deliver works for everyone.

As you pick users, choose ones that use different applications too. (This is one of the instances where using one of the software-based assessment tools really helps.) Even though you think you've thoroughly tested all the applications you'll use in your DaaS environment, users work with their applications much differently than you would. Your testing probably amounts to installing the app, clicking around, shrugging, and saying, "Yep, that one works," as you check it off your spreadsheet. But the users will find the little things that they need to do their job that you might have overlooked.

Infrastructure

We've talked about the specific network implications of running DaaS so far, like connecting to internal applications and ensuring your infrastructure can handle the additional traffic (another thing assessment tools can help with), but there's a lot of housekeeping we need to address as part of a migration.

For instance, are all of your DaaS users "remote" users now that their desktops are no longer hosted in your office? In other words, if their desktops and their files are all in the cloud, when they come into your office, how are they different from any other user working from home or a coffee shop? Really they're just using your network for their internet connection.

On the other hand, once they connect to their DaaS desktop, they're on "your" network at the DaaS provider, complete with access to your domain controllers, file servers, and applications. So who cares what the local network near their device is like? Or is this just another issue of semantics? With DaaS, who cares who's local and who's remote? The bigger distinction in your life probably is "DaaS" versus "traditional."

Another interesting infrastructure consideration is that if you switch all of a site's users to DaaS, and if you move your file servers and domain controller to the DaaS provider, do you need to maintain any servers at that office location? The users just need their clients and internet access, right? You can replace the entire server room with a network switch and a firewall (and maybe a WAN accelerator appliance).

Finally, don't forget that moving to DaaS means that you're going to be much more reliant on your network than before. Sure, we've spent plenty of time talking about the speed of your office's internet connection, but what about the internal LAN?

Most of us don't think twice about that because LANs are fast, right? That's true for wired networks, but have you seen what happens to a WiFi network with more than a dozen or so connections? Even the most modern 802.11n or 802.11ac networks can quickly get bogged down, especially when all the users are accessing continuous streams of remoting protocol session data.

Fortunately there are solutions to this. Companies like Aruba, Meru, Ruckus Wireless, and Xirrus have WiFi access points specifically designed for high numbers of simultaneous wireless LAN users. (Remember that if you tell users they can bring in whatever devices they want, chances are you're going to get three devices—a phone, a tablet, and a laptop—per user on your network. That means your 1997-era Cisco Aironet access points aren't going to cut it anymore!)

The final infrastructure thing we'll say here is that while a lot of DaaS providers talk about how your users can access their desktops via mobile 3G and 4G networks, our experience has been *very* hit or miss with this. One thing a lot of people don't realize is that those bandwidth claims are for ideal conditions with a full signal. But in actuality, when you're out in the world moving around, being blocked by buildings and trees, and switching towers, we found some user experiences to be lacking. (Of course this depends on your expectations and the nature of your applications.) We even found large differences among providers in the same city—it really comes down to how widely deployed their towers are *and* how many customers they have in that area. The 3G and 4G networks also add 10 to 20ms of latency over WiFi connections, which is something you'll have to deal with. And since 3G and 4G networks are shared with, well, everyone, connections can get spotty when there are a lot of people in one place. So keep all this in mind if you decide that you'll go with DaaS and just give all your users 4G cards, because your users can't work if their connection isn't solid, and our experience has shown that it often won't be.

Migrating to DaaS

Okay, now it's time to cover what you do during the actual act of migrating users to their new DaaS environment. By and large this is going to look an awful lot like a regular desktop migration, especially if you've migrated to VDI before. Frankly, DaaS migrations are pretty similar to a traditional desktop migration unless you are using non-persistent desktops. (As we discussed early on, non-persistent is very complex, so with this type of migration you can imagine that user settings and applications don't easily translate.)

Pre-DaaS migration checklist

We have a massive list of 204 questions to ask your DaaS provider in the appendix of this book, so definitely take a look at that to make sure you've covered everything before embarking on your migration.

Regarding the migration itself, here's what we hope you'd know before you get started:

- Do you know why you are moving to DaaS?
- Which users will you migrate? How will you notify them?
- What have you told your users? Do they understand that the network will affect their desktop's performance?
- Do the users know how to switch back and forth between their DaaS and local environments?
- Do you have a plan to get the new client software out to the users?
- Do the users know who they can call if they get confused?
- Do you have timelines you have to hit? (Shut down the old servers at 6 p.m. Get cloud-based file servers online by 9 a.m. the next day. Start with users, etc.)
- What is your rollback plan if the migration fails?
- How will you measure success? (Do it over the weekend—if users don't complain by 10 a.m. Monday, you win!)
- Is your provider on standby for tech support? Do they know you're migrating live users over?

Assuming you have answers to all of the above, now it's time to migrate. As we've mentioned already, this migration is no small task. This is a full-on desktop migration as complex (if not more complex) than any you've done in the past. In addition to the data and files and everything else we've looked at so far, let's talk about how you migrate two important things we haven't touched on yet: your users' settings and your desktop applications.

Migrating users' Windows settings

Let's first look at how you're going to get all your users' settings from their existing computers up to their new DaaS desktops. When we say "user settings," we're talking about the stuff that's in the Windows user profile, like the Microsoft Word custom dictionary, Outlook signatures, and UI tweaks that users can't live without (kitty cursors and whatnot). While some are obviously more business-critical than others, having to rebuild any of these from scratch would be annoying to both the users and the people on the help desk who have to receive the calls.

The problem we have with migrating settings—and this goes for any migration—is that out of the box, each user's settings, applications, and Windows OS are all combined into a single monolithic block: the user's Windows instance. So ideally we need a way to break out the user settings so we can migrate them on their own. One way to do that is with one of the aforementioned user environment management (UEM) products. These abstract user settings from the OS, making it possible for you as the admin to manage each setting on a per-user level (or per group, machine, network segment, OS type, device type—whatever!).

So if you already use a UEM solution, congratulations! You're in the migration fast lane. If not, you're pretty much stuck migrating to DaaS the same way you'd migrate between any two desktops—traditional or virtual. You're probably familiar with Microsoft's User State Migration Tool (USMT) or its GUI counterpart, the Windows Migration Assistant. If not, look them up. They're your best friends now!

That said, given the added management flexibility of UEM solutions, you should consider introducing them if you haven't already, even as part of the migration. (Yeah, we're aware that we warned you not to do too much at once, but these UEM products are great. AppSense, RES Software, Scense, Tricerat, Norskale, or Liquidware Labs are good places to start.) Moving forward, this compartmentalization of Windows will be key, especially as you move away from delivering full Windows desktops to delivering single Windows applications that may come together for the user from different locations. (And with UEM tools, you can manage your traditional, VDI, DaaS, and RDSH desktops and applications from multiple locations—all in the same way.)

Our last bit of advice here is that you should be deliberate about what you move from your users' existing desktops to their DaaS desktops. This applies whether you're using a UEM product or not. The temptation there is to just move their entire user profile up to the new DaaS environment, but the last thing you want is to gunk up your finely tuned DaaS image with a bunch of legacy garbage that nobody needs. (Do you really need those GroupWise mail profile registry keys anymore?)

Applications

While we're on the subject of compartmentalizing things, let's talk about application migrations. We've taken care of the application settings by using the techniques described above, but we still have to address the applications themselves. You've got two things you need to focus on:

1. Making sure the applications work.
2. Getting the right applications to the right users.

If you're using persistent desktop images for your DaaS environment, none of this should be any different from what you're doing today with your physical desktops. If you're using an application virtualization solution like App-V or ThinApp, keep using it for DaaS. If you're using SCCM and Altiris, keep it up. All your packages, groups, and management consoles should work the same way, apart from any server location changes for back-end components you might have moved to DaaS. Easy, right?

Now if you don't have an existing application virtualization or packaging/delivery solution, that's a different story. Without such a solution, you are probably used to building bespoke PCs based on a base or departmental image. You could do the same for DaaS, although all that image management becomes a real pain in the neck. But if you're used to that method, maybe you're okay with it.

It's also possible that your DaaS provider has some kind of preferred application management solution. This could be one of the application virtualization or packaging solutions mentioned above or a product like FSLogix, which can show or hide applications that are already installed in an image on a per-user basis. Or it could be a solution that uses layering, like Unidesk, VMware Horizon Mirage, or Moka5.

We mentioned layering earlier, but in case you're not familiar with the term, the short explanation is that it lets you compose unique disk images for users based on uniquely addressable "layer" disk images. Much like a layer cake, you'd have a base OS layer, one or more application layers, and a user layer all assembled dynamically when a desktop boots. When you want to add, remove, or change an application, you assign (or revoke) a layer for the user(s).

Several of the DaaS providers we spoke with have deals with layering vendors and make such products available in their DaaS environments. If your DaaS provider doesn't have a go-to solution, you can buy these products on your own and use them in your DaaS environment. Either way, these solutions, while outside the scope of this book, are generally pretty awesome and work well in DaaS environments.

All of this falls into the category of "there are a lot of ways to manage applications in Windows," and while we don't want you to go crazy changing too much when you go to DaaS, this migration might be a good time to change up the way you're delivering and exposing your Windows apps to your users.

What about P2V-ing the traditional desktops?

For those of you not familiar with P2V, which stands for Physical-to-Virtual, it's the process of making a disk image from an existing physical machine and converting it to a disk image for a virtual machine. P2V is typically used for servers. It's an easy way to convert a rackful of physical servers to a bunch of server VMs for a new virtual environment.

That said, there are situations where companies have actually used P2V for their VDI migration, creating hundreds of persistent VDI virtual machines from their existing physical desktop PCs.

Does this sound crazy? Maybe. But if you already have a well-managed physical PC environment that you like and you just want to move the PCs to VDI or DaaS, then why not? Heck, you could probably use P2V to do your whole DaaS migration in a single weekend! (You'd still have to make a few changes in each VM, like installing the VDI agents and stuff, but it sure is a lot easier than building everything from scratch!)

P2V-ing your desktop environment to VDI or DaaS was impossible a few years ago, but thanks to recent advances in storage technologies that can automatically identify and consolidate duplicated storage blocks across VMs, using P2V for your DaaS migration is actually possible now.

Most people choose not to do this though, usually because they want to use their DaaS migration as a chance to clean up their desktops and start fresh. But as a general migration concept, we like the idea. (For the record, we asked every DaaS provider we talked to about this, and none of them said that anyone had P2V-ed their machines. Some of them said the idea is crazy, but others were like, "Eh? Yeah, I guess that would work. We have no problem with it.")

The 'Typical' DaaS Migration Process

While there are certainly some technologically sleek methods for migrating your desktops, the general consensus is that your DaaS migration should be fairly process-oriented rather than "rip it and stick it." Most DaaS migrations look something like this:

1. The DaaS provider hands you one of their standard base images based on the version of the OS you've agreed to. (Actually, they will probably just give you access to a VM running in their cloud based on the fresh image.)
2. You do all the customizations you want and pass it back to the DaaS provider. ("Passing it back" in this case is you just let them know that you're done with it.)
3. The DaaS provider runs some basic optimization scripts on it so it works in their environment. (As we wrote before, there's nothing magical about the scripts, and you can absolutely find out what they're doing to optimize the image. It's just something they typically do to make sure things run as smoothly as possible in their environment.)
4. The DaaS provider adds your image into their system.
5. You configure your user accounts to assign which users to which image.
   - If you're using persistent images, this image will be the starting point for each user, but whatever users change is saved in their image. So over time each image ends up being different.
   - If you're using non-persistent images, this image is that shared image that each user's desktop gets reset to each time the user logs out.
6. Most customers typically run both environments (the old traditional desktop and the new DaaS desktop) in parallel for awhile. As the admin, you might choose to hide the original desktop from users so they're not inclined to use it, or so they're not confused by this "other" Start menu. After a certain length of time has passed and everyone has reached a comfort level, you can take the original desktops away or convert them into thin clients.

User Acceptance

Ahh . . . crazy, crazy users. They're like children. Just when you think you've childproofed your home, your kid comes walking out of your bedroom with a cigar he found in your underwear drawer.

"What's this, Daddy?"
<Sigh> "Umm . . . it's, uh, gum? Yeah, gum! It's Daddy's gum!"

Users always find ways to do all sorts of oddball things that we as admins can't figure out because we tend to view them as helpless creatures of habit. If the slightest thing changes on their desktop, they're confused. But they spend all day, every day using their desktops, so if there's a way to discover something we didn't think about it, chances are they'll eventually stumble upon it.

Gabe, in his current job as a blogger and speaker, actually got a call from some random person asking if he could help him log in to his Citrix desktop. Apparently this guy (an end user, mind you) googled his problem, found BrianMadden.com, clicked on the Contact Us page, and called Gabe. (This is why Brian does not list his phone number on the website.) Gabe told the guy that he should probably call someone at his company, but the guy said he "hates calling his worthless help desk." This story is 100% true. Users are weird.

So one of the goals of your DaaS environment should be to avoid pissing off your users so much that they randomly call bloggers they find on the internet. You do this by making sure your users buy in to the new system. This means understanding how they use their desktops and trying hard to replicate what they have now while still managing to get the features you want. Fixing a problem or removing a limitation your users have—or didn't even know they had—is a bonus.

Part of this involves training. If we just show up one day to set up the new client software, show the users their new desktop, and then turn around and leave, within minutes they'll call the help desk asking why there are two Start menus or where their grandkids' pictures went. Moving desktops to DaaS and changing the way users access and interact with them requires a serious training effort before rollout.

If you're lucky enough to work at a company that has a corporate IT trainer that isn't you, add that person to your pilot group so he or she can share hands-on knowledge heading into training sessions. (And if you're really bold, put your most, um, "challenging" users in the pilot too so that you can identify any serious issues and fix them beforehand.)

The biggest roadblock to user acceptance, though, is not paying attention to users' needs ahead of time. If your users are used to having a dual display setup with iTunes installed so they can listen to their music (why aren't they just using their phone?), along with fast performance when using and switching between applications and the ability to browse YouTube during lunch, taking any of that away will make them hate the new DaaS. Sure, there's always some pushback anytime something changes, but if more than a handful of users are discontent, they will revolt, and it only takes a few managers banging on the CIO's door before you get called to the carpet.

It's not that you have to cater to every single user's needs, but you should understand at a departmental level what your users are trying to do. Meet with the managers and ask what they need their users to have. Add them to the pilot even. Just be more in touch with your users than the desktop admin for that random internet person who called Gabe out of the blue. If necessary, bribe them with pizza and beer. (Or spend the $400 to buy each of them an iPad so they can do their Facebook and YouTube stuff and your DaaS doesn't have to support it—and your users will love you forever because you bought them iPads.)

The only group that will push back until their arms fall off are the laptop users. If you think you can convince them to use a DaaS desktop that lives online when they have Office and a browser and all their files that work offline in front of them, you're crazy. (Time for IT management for you!) As we discussed before, even though 3G and 4G networks are pervasive today, laptop users are accustomed to doing the one thing no DaaS, VDI, or RDSH solution can (or will ever) be able to provide: offline use. Honestly you're probably better off not even trying to convert laptop users (unless their laptops never leave their desks).

So pay attention to your users, give them the clients they need to access the desktops with the same fidelity they had before, train them on the new system, and completely ignore the laptop users, and you'll be in great shape as you move over to DaaS!

17. Quitting DaaS

No matter how much homework you do, how many providers you audition, or how many meetings you have, there are just some situations where DaaS doesn't work out. DaaS is moving the execution of users' Windows desktops away from their desks and into some far-off data center, so there's lots of room for technical issues to arise, which can stop a DaaS project dead in its tracks.

There are also plenty of less technical reasons that could derail a DaaS project—either before it ever begins or after you've already gone through the pain to get there. For instance, your relationship with the provider could sour. Or maybe they can't scale up fast enough to continue providing a consistent experience for you as they bring on new customers. Or, as much as we don't want to think of it, perhaps they go out of business.

So in this chapter we want to look at why DaaS projects fail, why people choose to quit using DaaS, and what you need to do to prepare for those possibilities.

Why Do People Quit DaaS?

DaaS projects are often judged based on the users' experiences. After all, the users are the kings, and if they don't buy in, eventually their managers will be mad. When the managers are mad, the directors get mad. And since crap can only go so high before it starts rolling back downhill, it will eventually work its way back to you.

The user experience is so easily affected by so many different externalities (network, storage, compute, clients, and so on) that it's often hard to pinpoint the source of the problem. Sure, there's no shortage of tools that can help with that, but if enough people complain right out of the gate, your first instinct is usually a knee-jerk reaction like, "Let's double the number of vCPUs each user has," or something equally as rash and uninformed. In on-premises VDI environments, those issues can usually be addressed because you own the architecture. It's not as easy with DaaS, and even if the DaaS provider can throw more hardware at a problem, they're just going to pass those charges onto you in the form of a higher monthly cost per desktop.

That said, let's take a look at the most common reasons people quit using DaaS, including:

- Cost
- Trying to do too much
- Other "standard" VDI issues

Cost

Unfortunately cost is still one of the big reasons that people quit DaaS. A lot of this happens because customers are told that DaaS will be way cheaper than something else. Sometimes this happens because the DaaS provider flat-out says, "DaaS is going to be cheaper." Other times it's because the customer has "proven" to themselves that DaaS will be cheaper with a flawed cost model.

This happens for the reasons we outlined in the "Understanding the True Cost of DaaS" section of this book, including manipulating soft costs or leaving out (or "reallocating") some key expenses. Our research found that labor costs are frequently left out of DaaS cost models because nobody really knows how much labor will be involved in the migration process and how much management work customers will still have to do once they get to DaaS.

So when all the resources, time, and money are tallied up, companies are surprised to learn that their DaaS environment costs a lot more than the $35 per user per month they anticipated. That right there is a reason many pull the plug and give DaaS a black eye to anyone they talk to.

If cost is your main concern, keep in mind that you're not moving to DaaS because you want to save money (just like you wouldn't move to VDI to save money). DaaS is about adding features, flexibility, manageability, accessibility, and so on, above and beyond your existing traditional desktop capabilities.

Sure, DaaS can be cheaper than on-premises VDI, since the DaaS provider can take better advantage of economies of scale than a typical company. They have the expertise and the infrastructure to do great things at a huge scale while spreading that cost around to all their customers. But if you're just going to DaaS to save money, you're going to be disappointed, and that could ultimately lead to a killed project.

Doing too much

Another reason people quit DaaS is that they've tried to bite off more than they can chew. We sort of mentioned this earlier when talking about which companies make good candidates for DaaS. If you're already familiar with VDI because you're running it internally and you're just sick of it, then you're already familiar with the concepts that surround DaaS and there shouldn't be too many surprises. You already know about things like image management, templates, updates, application virtualization, profiles, and user experience management.

Those companies that have no experience with VDI are at a disadvantage when it comes to DaaS because they're walking into unfamiliar territory without any real experience with the solution they're about to adopt. (Again, we highly recommend reading one of our VDI books if you have no experience with it.) In

196 • DESKTOPS AS A SERVICE

these cases people don't know what questions to ask or what to look for. They've heard about concepts like single images, layering, and personalization, among others, which are all pretty easy to understand at a high level. But when it comes time to deploy, they realize that it's hard and that DaaS is just Desktops as a Service, not Desktop Engineering as a Service. (Remember you can get that service too, but you're going to spend more than $35 per user per month.)

You might be thinking, "Okay, I have all these traditional persistent desktop PCs and my environment is chaos. I want all the nice things like single-image management and app virtualization and layering and user environment management, but I don't want to get in the weeds of VDI so I'm just going to pay someone for DaaS." If this is you, then you are not ready for DaaS, and if you try to move to DaaS, you're in for a world of hurt and will probably end up switching away from it because it doesn't meet your needs. Or, at a minimum, you might switch from shared non-persistent images to persistent images. But in that case you might think, "Well, if DaaS isn't making my desktops easier to manage, why am I doing DaaS?"

This means you're not ready, and you'll quit DaaS because you're frustrated.

Not being ready for VDI

The final big reason that people quit DaaS is because they're not ready for VDI. Or, more technically, they're not ready for the concept of remote Windows desktops replacing local Windows desktops. This can be for any of the reasons we outlined in the VDI chapters at the beginning of this book, including network performance issues or limitations such as not being able to use DaaS desktops while offline.

We've seen plenty of people who have tried DaaS and quit not because of any DaaS-specific issue, but because of classic VDI issues like these. They just weren't good fits for VDI.

When Do You Pull the Plug?

If you realize that DaaS is not right for you, the timing of when you pull the plug will directly affect the pain you'll feel. We hope that many people will choose not to use DaaS after reading this book—not because we don't love DaaS (because we do!), but because we want everyone who tries DaaS to be successful. So if we can cut off a project that is doomed for failure before it begins, we'll feel pretty good for helping someone avoid that pain.

If you decide to try a DaaS proof of concept or pilot and then realize it's not right for you, you're still one of the lucky ones. Abandoning DaaS at this point is still relatively painless. (That's another reason it's important to pick some "difficult" users for your pilot. If you just pick the easy users to ensure your pilot's success, you've just pushed your pain down the road to a point where it will hurt even more and be more expensive.)

But if you make it all the way into production before realizing DaaS isn't going to work for you, you've got a tough road ahead. How easy is it going to be to roll back to your environment? Do you go to a different DaaS provider? Do you build up your own on-premises VDI environment? Do you roll out Windows onto traditional desktop PCs? Either way, it's not going to be pretty.

You Need an Exit Plan

While doing research for this book, a guy who works at a DaaS provider told us, "I'm surprised by how few customers move to DaaS without having an exit plan. If I were a CIO, I would *never* move into the cloud without having a plan for how I would move back out." We agree completely. Even if you trust a company implicitly, how can you give them all of your desktops—which your users depend on to do all their work every day—without putting together a plan to get them back?

There are two reasons you'd need such a plan. The first is what we're calling a "controlled exit," which would be used when you want to leave a provider either because DaaS isn't working out for you and you want to bring your desktops back in house, or because you're not happy with that provider and you'd like to switch to a different one.

The second would be an "uncontrolled exit" plan, which you'd need in case something happened at the provider and they couldn't be your DaaS host anymore. Ideally you'd have some heads up if they were going out of business, but it's also possible that you wake up one day and all the desktops are just gone.

So let's take a look at how you can plan for each type of exit.

Controlled exit strategy

The controlled exit strategy is one you can talk with your provider about ahead of time. Sure, they're not going to want you to leave, but they have to know it's a possibility at some point, and if they're confident in their abilities, they will be happy to work out a plan with you. (Actually if they're not supportive of an exit strategy, we'd take that as a warning sign.) Remember that you're the customer (or potential customer), so you're in command of this relationship.

The most important thing to address is your data. Your primary concern is where your data is and how you can download it or otherwise get it back. Your secondary concern should be that if you decide to leave your provider, what's their plan for securely deleting your data once you get it back? You want to make sure it's not sitting around somewhere where someone else could get their hands on it.

Find out what your options are for getting your data, both in terms of how it will be transferred to you and what format it will be in. Are they going to give you an FTP login to some website? Will they give you disk images? Will they burn DVDs and mail them to you? (Is that still a thing?) You need to know this ahead of time.

Once your data is taken care of, you need to think about your desktops. Since we're talking about controlled exits here, if you're planning on moving to another DaaS provider (or to in-house VDI) that runs on the same platform as your current provider, you might be able to directly transfer your disk images to the new environment. (If you're planning to move to in-house VDI, just be sure to take a good hard look at why the DaaS project failed and why you think you can be successful with in-house VDI.)

If you're switching to a different platform altogether, the images won't prove to be all that helpful. The virtual machines will likely be incompatible, and you'll end up doing so much work to make them fit that it's probably worthwhile to just start from scratch so you don't build in any vestigial, resource-sucking bits from the image's past life.

The big challenge here is going to be if you're using non-persistent images. Sure, the master image might be easy to get back, but what about any layering solutions, app virtualization, or user environment components? Normally these aren't the kinds of things you'd pay much attention to, since they fall under the umbrella of DaaS plumbing, but in this case it affects your exit migration.

Then again, one of the beauties of non-persistent desktops is that since they're reset after each use, there's nothing of value on them that you need to worry about for recovery purposes. You just need to make sure that you can get all the other components—your application packages, your UEM database, your scripts, and so on—to rebuild your desktop environment somewhere else.

Uncontrolled exit strategy

This is the emergency plan that we hope you never have to use, but since your DaaS provider is a separate company at a separate location, really you have no idea whether, when, if, or how an uncontrolled exit might happen. Remember we talked about how this could be as random as the FBI raiding your provider because one of their other customers was doing something illegal. (This could affect you and all their other customers, since the feds could potentially back their truck up to the data center and seize the provider's SAN.)

You should ask your provider if they have a plan for this scenario. Don't let them tell you it's far-fetched—we're including it in this book because it is a real situation that has happened before!

Much of the preparation for an uncontrolled exit is the same as for a controlled one. The difference is that with an uncontrolled exit, you'll need to be proactive in maintaining everything you need at a secondary location (in addition to your primary DaaS provider). That location can be another cloud provider, where you only buy storage services to hold your backups, or it can be in a location on your own premises.

This can be as simple as one of those consumer NAS devices you can buy from someone like Buffalo or Drobo. You can get several terabytes of capacity for just a few hundred dollars and keep it under your desk. Of course you'd never use this thing for production access, but you could just have it trickle down files from the cloud so you always have a synced copy of your data onsite. You could even configure it so the syncing operations happen at night when the office is empty. (Just make sure you factor in any data transfer costs from your DaaS provider.)

The most elegant solution, should some catastrophic event separate you from your desktops, is to spread your workload around to multiple DaaS providers. We're not statisticians, but the odds of two providers going out of business or being raided at the exact same time is roughly 13 million times less than it happening to a single company. (It's a ballpark number.)

Spreading the load around gives you the added benefit of load balancing, not to mention the ability for users to connect to the closest data center and the ability to place data where it might legally be required to live. The downside is that you still have to figure out how to replicate data between providers.

At the end of the day you don't want to find yourself in a situation where you have just one provider that has disappeared. You've moved to DaaS entirely, converted your PCs to thin clients (or replaced them outright with thin clients), and changed the way you manage desktops from top to bottom. There's no magic reset button to make it all go back to the old way overnight. Even if you ordered every PC you could find locally, you'll never get back up and running in time to make a dent in the amount of pain you're feeling.

If you're in a situation where this could happen and you can't (or won't) add another provider, perhaps you can establish a comfort level by evaluating the company financials on a regular basis or keeping tabs on your provider's employee activity (have you had a new contact person each month?). Again, this only works for smaller companies, but those are the ones we're worried about. This situation isn't as much of a problem if you're getting your desktops directly from a large vendor like VMware, Microsoft, or Amazon. If they go out of business, you've likely got bigger fish to fry.

Summary

If you decide DaaS doesn't work for you, take the time to figure out why. It's a worthwhile endeavor that can help you avoid issues in the future and probably point out areas where your current desktop management strategy falls short. Plus, no matter how much planning you do, there is always going to be the risk that your DaaS project fails for one reason or another. Make sure you have a plan should that situation arise, whether expected or not, and you'll be ready for just about anything.

18. Alternatives to DaaS

At this point you've made it almost all the way through a book about DaaS. It's possible that based on what you've been reading, you're thinking, "Yikes! This DaaS thing is *not* for me!" It's also possible that your boss told you that you need to go to DaaS, you've read this book and don't agree, and now you need to know what your other options are.

So what do you do now? Do you wait it out and then try again in a year or two? Or is this more of a permanent thing? The answer depends on what your reasons are for not wanting to do DaaS today.

Perhaps you just can't muster up enough trust in the providers, which is totally acceptable as long as it's not based on some misguided "the cloud is never going to take off" philosophy. Cloud is here and is already taking in areas of your IT even if you choose to ignore it. Dropbox, Gmail, Salesforce, and many, many other things that we can't even name are infiltrating your systems and your users' computing environments today, and they will only continue to grow.

If you're on board with embracing the cloud but still have the issue of finding a trusted provider, you're not alone. The simple fact is that for many companies, it will take time to become comfortable with the cloud, and migrations will be focused on singular purposes rather than en masse. The cloud will continue to pick up steam over time, though, following a trajectory similar to that of server virtualization (which people also didn't trust in its formative years, albeit for different reasons). If trust is your issue, you have time. Circle back in a year or two and see if the cloud matches your company's sensibilities then.

If you still want to do data center-hosted desktops in the meantime, there's always in-house VDI and/or RDSH.

Or, finally, if you've decided that desktops in the data center is just not for you at all, that's fine too. You can still take advantage of many of the technologies we've talked about throughout this book to better manage your traditional desktops.

So now let's take a look at three alternatives to DaaS: on-premises VDI, RDSH, and traditional desktops.

VDI: The Original DaaS

We've already established that DaaS is just VDI that you pay someone else to implement and manage, so one of the alternatives is obviously going to be to do it yourself. We discussed VDI earlier in the book, so no need to rehash everything, but there are still a few things we can touch on here.

If you pay any attention to the cloud computing marketing, you won't have to wait long before hearing the term "private cloud." Soon after that you might hear the phrase "internal DaaS." Let's make one thing crystal clear: There is no such thing as internal DaaS. That is called VDI.

The only way we'll accept the use of "internal DaaS" is if you decide that on-premises VDI is the right solution for you but your boss insists you have to use "DaaS." In that case, yeah, call your VDI "internal DaaS." (Actually, if you want to really make your boss happy, tell him or her that you're going to do "DaaS in the private cloud," and then just build VDI like you normally would.)

Apart from that, "internal DaaS" should be thrown in the buzzword trash bin next to "SaaS-ify" and "phablet."

That said, some of the platforms that DaaS providers use are also available to private companies to use to host their own on-premises VDI environments. Citrix's XenDesktop platform is leveraged by many DaaS providers and of course available for on-premises VDI deployments. We're also excited to see what happens with VMware, since we expect that their on-premises Horizon View product will merge with their cloud-based Desktone product to provide a single platform that can be used by DaaS providers and for in-house VDI deployments. Both Nimdesk and dinCloud also make their platforms available for on-premises DaaS-like VDI deployments.

Our point is that if you want to build an on-premises VDI environment, you don't need to focus on making a DaaS platform yourself. You can simply use the existing VDI technology. There are several companies with mature systems at various price points and feature sets, including:

- Citrix XenDesktop
- VMware Horizon View
- Microsoft Remote Desktop Services
- Dell vWorkspace
- Virtual Bridges VERDE
- Ericom PowerTerm WebConnect
- Desktopsites Konect Elite
- Leostream Connection Broker

The challenge when building your own VDI instead of DaaS, as we've mentioned several times already, is you have to figure out why you think on-premises VDI will work for you when DaaS won't. There are several acceptable reasons, including that you don't have to worry about finding a provider to trust and you don't have to worry as much about bandwidth to your users in the office. Just read our other book first!

RDSH-based Solutions

You've seen references to Remote Desktop Session Host (RDSH) a few times throughout this book, but if you're still reading this chapter, you may not be as familiar with it as other solutions. No problem! Remember that RDSH is the server-based technology from Microsoft that allows multiple users to be simultaneously logged on to a single Windows Server, with each user getting his or her own "session." This has been called server-based computing and Terminal Server in the past, but we today use the term RDSH to describe them all.

We also use the terms RDSH to describe the environments powered by third-party platforms. Citrix XenApp (formerly Citrix Presentation Server, formerly Citrix MetaFrame) is the most popular, but there's also Dell vWorkspace, Ericom PowerTerm WebConnect, Propalms TSE, and 2X ApplicationServer.

The various RDSH-based solutions—either as vanilla Microsoft-only RDSH or RDSH with a third-party add-on—can be used to deliver either full Windows desktop sessions or single seamless Windows applications via the same protocols (HDX/ICA, Remote-FX, PC-over-IP, etc.) as VDI or DaaS. And as we've said throughout this book, RDSH-based solutions are one of the options that many DaaS providers offer to their customers. (From an end user's standpoint, RDSH-based solutions look no different than VDI or single-user Windows Server desktops.)

For years (since the 1990s) RDSH was the only option for delivering remote Windows environments, so it has the advantage of being proven technology that a lot of people are already familiar with. Citrix has sold something like 100 million licenses of XenApp, and almost every single Fortune 500 company has at least some XenApp in their environment, so an alternative to DaaS could very realistically be, "Why don't we just use our existing XenApp environment?"

RDSH-based solutions have historically been less expensive on a per-user basis than VDI, since you can put multiple users on the same instance of Windows, though now that hypervisor technology has matured, the density benefits of RDSH are minimized. Customers still like it though, because with RDSH, you get "automatic" non-persistent image sharing (since all your users on the RDSH server share the same RDSH image).

So if you're thinking about an alternative to non-persistent DaaS that you want to run in-house, RDSH could be an answer. And if you already have an RDSH-based solution up and running, it might be much simpler to extend that for your new users rather than fussing around with DaaS or VDI. But the same caveat from VDI above also applies here: If DaaS isn't going to work for you, why not, and why do you think RDSH would?

Ultimately, though, we love RDSH. We (along with many others in the industry) have been working with it for seventeen years, and there's a huge wealth of industry knowledge around it. So if you're just looking to host some remote Windows desktops or applications for your users and you want to build something internally, RDSH could be the way to go.

Traditional Desktop PCs

The final alternative to DaaS is to just keep using your traditional desktop PCs and laptops. This solution has the advantage that the performance is the same regardless of how well the internet is working, and of course your laptop users can fully work offline.

Throughout this book we've talked about various Windows desktops "modernization" technologies and products that transform the way you manage desktops to make them more manageable. (We mean things like application virtualization, user environment management, centralized patch management, and so on.) As we've said again and again, these technologies are not exclusive to DaaS—you can use all of them to change the way you manage your traditional desktop PCs and laptops too.

We said that many VDI (and DaaS) projects fail because companies try to do too much at once. They want to get the benefits of VDI or DaaS (like access from anywhere and flexibility) while also getting the benefits of a better-managed Windows desktop.

So if you're looking for the benefits of a better-managed desktop but you don't necessarily need the benefits of VDI or DaaS, then applying app virtualization, user environment management,

208 • DESKTOPS AS A SERVICE

and central patch management to your existing Windows desktop PCs and laptops might make more sense than going to DaaS.

Keep in mind that there are also several "next generation" desktop management products that leverage layering and virtualization running directly on users' desktops and laptops. For example, Moka5 LivePC and BareMetal, Citrix XenClient, and VMware Horizon Mirage all give you a central management console you can use to update, manage, patch, and remotely wipe your desktops and laptops—all without the downsides of remote computing.

Another option is that if you're looking for the benefit of "I want someone else to manage my desktop environment," you could consider finding a managed service provider or desktop outsourcing company that can take on the full management of your existing physical desktops and laptops. This way you can get out of the desktop management business without the downsides of remote computing.

Remember that DaaS is Desktops as a Service, not Desktop Management and Engineering as a Service, so if you want to use DaaS to outsource the management of your desktop estate, you're probably going to have to pay $35 to $50 per user per month just for the DaaS, and then another $50 to $300 per user per month for the management of the desktops. Hiring a service provider to manage your existing desktops might be cheaper than DaaS and have less of an impact to your overall business.

What Are You Trying to Do in the First Place?

In order to truly decide whether DaaS is the right solution for you versus one of the alternatives like VDI, RDSH, or sticking with traditional desktops, you have to ask yourself what you're trying to do in the first place. Are you simply trying to ride the buzz because you can't turn your head without hearing something about DaaS? Is your CIO breathing down your neck, saying you have to do this thing because his or her CIO buddies on the golf course are also doing it? (We all know that the only thing CIOs do is golf and attend conferences, and when they're golfing the only thing they talk about is what's going on at work, right?)

Remember that VDI and DaaS are about remote computing. They're about moving users' Windows desktops and applications to a data center. Remote computing has advantages like the ability to connect from any device, but it has disadvantages like not working with no or slow internet connections.

If that's what you want to do, and you want to do that without the headache and expense of building and running a VDI environment on your own, then DaaS is for you.

On the other hand, if you're just looking to find a better way to manage your desktops, DaaS may not be the answer. It *could* be the answer, but you (or your DaaS or managed service provider) will have to do a lot of engineering to transform the way you deliver desktops in order to get that. That could be something you do at the same time that you move to DaaS, or you could just make those management changes and keep on using your existing desktops and laptops.

At the end of the day you have to ask yourself what you're trying to achieve. Figure out your *actual* goals, and then decide whether DaaS is the answer. DaaS is only going to be a small sliver of the market for the next few years, so if you don't go to DaaS today, there's plenty of time to go there when it makes sense.

19. The Future of Windows and DaaS

We're going to wrap up this book by taking a look at the future of both of DaaS and Windows in general. After all, we're surrounded by this drumbeat of "Windows is dying." But is that even true? If so, does that mean that all this investment in DaaS is a waste? Or does it mean that you should *accelerate* your migration to DaaS?

Here's how we see this story playing out:

- Everywhere you turn, you hear that Windows is dying.
- In the enterprise, that's not exactly true. Legacy Windows desktop applications will be around forever.
- Historically, the Windows desktop has been the hub of end-user computing in the enterprise. This is changing into something else.
- We need a way to deliver our legacy Windows desktop applications into that "something else."

- That way could be VDI or DaaS.
- Microsoft might make this difficult.
- You still have to do something today.

Let's examine each of these in more detail.

Everywhere you turn, you hear that Windows is dying

Windows is dying. There, we said it. So if you haven't heard it before, you have now! The evidence is all around you. Just take a look in your own home. Even if you have a computer that runs Windows, what do you do with it? Facebook, Instagram, Gmail, YouTube, Netflix, Amazon, and so on. None of these things actually requires Windows. Sure, you might use Office, but if you didn't have the Windows version, would your life be altered that much by using a SaaS equivalent like Google Docs? Probably not. Heck, this entire book was written in Google Docs. (No joke!)

And what about your files on your Windows computer? Those are going away too. Do you store a bunch of Word docs locally? Nope! They're stored (or even created in) Google Drive. Music? In the iTunes cloud. Photos? In Flickr. Task list? Evernote. (Does that even have files?) Even those few remaining files are cloud-enabled via something like Dropbox or OneDrive so you can access them from your phone or tablet no matter where you are.

Sure, you might have one or two must-have Windows desktop applications—<cough> Visio <cough>—but the reality is you rely on far fewer than you did ten, five, or even three years ago. The importance of Windows in your life is dwindling.

It looks like the same is true in the enterprise. Ever since the release of Windows XP and Internet Explorer 6, companies have been trying to "webify" their applications. In hindsight it happened too early, and today many of us are still dealing with the ramifications of applications written for IE 6 that don't work on any other platform today. But after learning that lesson we just got wise to using more OS- and browser-independent solutions, so much so that many of our enterprise and line-of-business applications are actually being delivered from internal web servers now.

Even those stalwarts of the Windows desktop image, like Outlook and Office, are starting to find their way to the web. Office 365 is picking up a lot of steam, and the Outlook Web App in Exchange 2013 is almost better than using the actual Outlook desktop application to access email. So even on your work desktop, the percentage of applications that require Windows is diminishing.

The evidence is there, both at home and the office, that Windows is on the way out. It's been moving in that direction for years, and we don't expect that trend to stop.

'Dying' doesn't mean 'dead,' at least in the enterprise

Windows may be on its way out, but it's not dead yet. If it were, every employee of a large company would be carrying a Chromebook and this DaaS book wouldn't exist.

While it's true that the *percentage* of Windows desktop applications compared with apps in the cloud or on other platforms may be diminishing, the *number* of Windows desktop applications is still fairly high. Consider that fifteen years ago, a large enterprise might have had 300 apps, and all 300 of them were Windows apps. Seven years ago, they may have had 500 applications, of which 350 were Windows (the rest being web-based). Today, that number might be 600 apps or more, but there may still be 300 Windows applications in use. So while the number of Windows apps is still relatively high, the percentage of applications that are Windows-based is decreasing.

The main reason for this is that Windows desktops applications are so tightly ingrained into our enterprise processes that it will take decades to untangle them. We also have to deal with the fact that single Windows applications don't typically exist in a vacuum. How many times have you heard, "Oh yeah, we'd love to ditch Microsoft Office, but we can't because of all our add-ins and macros." It's not uncommon to find one Windows app that talks to another Windows app to generate reports, which uses Windows Excel OLE to generate charts, which prints to a special printer, which only has Windows drivers.

When you were new to desktop support and someone showed you how these apps worked, you probably thought, "What?! This is all held together with duct tape and chewing gum!" And here's the thing—you're right! It *is* all held together like some crazy Rube Goldberg machine, and unfortunately the person who originally set it up doesn't work there anymore. So it persists!

Industry pundits and CIO strategists tell you, "The future is the web! Users want iPads! You have to rewrite all these crappy legacy applications!" Sure, that's a nice plan, but we've heard it all before. Ten years ago we thought all the apps would be rewritten to Java or .Net web apps. Four years ago they were all going to be iOS apps. Today? Crazy Windows desktop apps persist.

So what makes us think we're going to move off these important Windows applications anytime soon? They've been around forever, and if it were easy to rewrite them for a new platform, that would have been done by now. (Actually we could say the mere fact that these Windows applications haven't been migrated yet—with all the other options out there—is proof in itself that they're going to be around for a long time. Heck, look at mainframe applications. How many enterprises still have those? And that technology's been "dead" for twenty-five years!)

So like it or not, Windows desktop applications are going to be a big part of the enterprise for years to come.

What about the Windows desktop?

Okay, so that's all well and good for Windows *applications*. But what about the actual Windows desktop itself?

Most of us don't appreciate the desktop's role as the hub of an end user's life. We can talk about how all these web apps and services are replacing Windows apps, and how they don't use traditional files because everything they store is in their own backend, but think about how that actually impacts a user's workflow. In that world where every application is a web app, a user has to know exactly where to look for everything, since each piece of data is tied specifically to an application.

A desktop, on the other hand, aggregates all of that for them, either natively or via plugins. Google Drive documents are integrated into searches, as are notes in Evernote, emails, and files in Dropbox and elsewhere. The ability to easily find files wherever they happen to be is a major role a desktop plays in a user's life.

The desktop also acts as the connecting linkage between all the moving parts of the different applications. This includes things like OLE, COM objects, workflows, scripting, printing, filing, moving, sharing—basically anything that one application does to interact with another, and it's something that happens more often than we think. (If you want an example of what your world would be like without this, buy a keyboard for your iPad and try to use it as your primary computer for a week. It's awful! Every application is 100% isolated from every other application, and apart from basic copying and pasting, there's nothing linking any of them together. It is not a good experience!)

Finally, the Windows desktop is a convenient place to hold users' settings, which are inherited by all of their applications. This is obvious for things like time zone and regionalization preferences, but remember it also applies to things like file locations. The Windows desktop provides a convenient default location whereby you just hit "save" and forget about it. And don't forget about the core services that one Windows application can provide to others, like email, contacts, and schedule management.

So while it's easy to see how we could move beyond Windows applications, what about the Windows desktop? What will become the new "hub" in a post-Windows world?

We need a way to deliver Windows applications into that new world

There's a lot of talk in our industry right now about portals and federated app environments and all sorts of other new age-y end-user environments. We're seeing early efforts with things like VMware Horizon Workspace and Citrix StoreFront, but at this stage in the game we're not sure whether anyone has a clear picture of exactly what that will look like.

We do know that this new environment will have to work on all devices, form factors, and operating systems. Furthermore, we know it will need to be a *native* experience on all of these devices. So it might be a keyboard- and mouse-based environment for desktop PCs and laptops, albeit one that feels like Windows on a Windows computer and Mac-like on a Mac. It should be a native iOS app on iPhones and iPads and a native Android app on Android devices. It should work perfectly on devices that are owned and controlled by companies and on employee-owned devices (BYOD).

We also know that this new environment should leverage all of the capabilities of each device and platform. It can't be something lame like, "Here's a web-based portal for your apps," since an iOS user would expect to access an app via a native app icon that knows who the user is rather than, "Open Safari, click on this link, log in, then click on the app you want to use."

Finally, this new end-user hub needs to be centrally controlled by the administrator, but in a way that abstracts the device from that process. As an administrator moving forward, you want to say, "This user needs Salesforce," and let the platform figure out what exactly that means for each device. You don't want to have to configure it like, "Okay, if you're on an iPad, you get the iOS Salesforce app, but if you're on a Mac, you get a web link." That's something that should be done once when an application is set up—not something that's manual for each user.

So how do we deliver our enterprise Windows applications into this new hub?

Tying in VDI and DaaS

The million-dollar question is, "Could VDI (and, by extension, DaaS) be one of the spokes that delivers Windows desktop applications into this future end-user computing hub?" We think yes.

In this future environment we might be talking about just delivering single windows from DaaS rather than delivering the entire Windows desktop environment. After all, the Windows desktop environment is the hub of yesterday, and the whole point of this future hub is that it's not Windows.

We understand, by the way, that the form factor of Windows desktop applications might not be the most ideal UI for every client device in the future. Sure, DaaS-delivered Windows applications will be perfectly usable via future devices that have keyboards and mice, but no amount of technological wizardry will make a Windows desktop application that was designed for a huge screen, keyboard, and mouse work well on an iPad. That's okay though, since this future doesn't force users to awkwardly use *all* their apps as Windows apps. Rather, you only need to force them to use the legacy apps that can only run on Windows.

When this comes to fruition, we'll see that Windows has become more of an application platform than a desktop environment. In that world, the Windows applications run on Windows desktop environments in some remote data center, and your users are able to remotely access the platform from whatever device they're on.

This transition isn't going to happen overnight. You'll have some users, using some devices, leveraging single seamless Windows applications coming from the cloud. You'll have other users who will require a full Windows desktop, whether it runs locally on their computer or is delivered remotely from the cloud. To make this happen, DaaS providers are creating solutions that deliver both seamless Windows applications and full desktops. You can continue to deliver full remote desktops to users who still need you to provide them with the "hub," while slowly transitioning over to an environment where you deliver Windows applications as standalone apps without the desktop wrapper. Eventually your remaining desktops will be zero, and the only Windows you'll care about managing is whatever you need to do to deliver those apps.

So how far in the future is this? We believe you have until somewhere around January 14, 2020. (A Tuesday, if you'd like to put in the time-off request now.) How can we be so sure? Simple! That's the day Microsoft will stop supporting Windows 7, meaning you have to be off of it by then.

Many CIOs believe that the Windows XP to Windows 7 migration that's fresh in most of our minds will be the last traditional migration they do. (Traditional in the sense that they have corporate-managed desktops and laptops throughout their company that they mass migrate to a new version of Windows.) If we look at the influence of the cloud (versus locally installed Windows applications), users' demands to work with devices that don't run

Windows, users' desire for mobility, and the fact that Microsoft has been forcing us into their way of doing desktops for the past twenty years, we can easily see why many people don't want "next time" to be the same as "last time."

So maybe by 2020 you'll have this new end-user computing hub that means you won't have to upgrade 500 million desktops and laptops from Windows 7 to Windows 10. Or maybe you will do another traditional upgrade. Either way, we know that you'll have to lean on your "Windows as middleware" platform to deliver all of your Windows desktop applications into that new world. This is where DaaS is a perfect fit.

By the way, Microsoft might make this difficult

As we've mentioned a few times already, since everything we're talking about in this book is about Microsoft Windows, you're totally at the mercy of Microsoft when it comes to what you can do. Even if you're using a third-party DaaS provider who has nothing to do with them, Microsoft's dark hand is involved in all aspects of your DaaS environment.

Microsoft has the total ability to, at their whim, make massive licensing or policy changes that could majorly (and instantaneously) affect your DaaS environment. For instance, Microsoft could change licensing to revoke the SPLA license for single-user instances of Windows Server in order to force customers to buy their own SA or VDA licenses.

Some argue this isn't likely, since doing so would undermine their long-standing position that Server and Desktop editions of Windows are fundamentally different. But hey, if Microsoft is forced to keep fighting for relevance over the next few years, who knows what they could do? Remember this is the company who raised the price of Remote Desktop Services CALs last year in response to the trend of companies buying per-user licenses to support multiple devices per user. This is the company who suddenly decided in 2008 that you had to have an RDS CAL for single user sessions, instantly charging for something that had been "free" since 2000. This is the company who announced double-digit price increases for SPLA for both 2014 and 2015.

So Microsoft has an established history of changing their license policies and pricing to support their bottom line. Combine that with the fact that they have a new CEO and declining market share and who knows what could happen?

Of course it's *possible* that Microsoft could actually make changes for the better. Maybe they'll wake up one day and decide that not allowing a Windows client OS to be covered by SPLA is asinine? Or that not allowing service providers to share hardware between SA customers goes against their "green" image, since it forces the providers to run extra, underutilized servers? (While both of those seem great at first, imagine the chaos that would cause in the DaaS market? What if you spent months designing around Microsoft's licensing restrictions and then they go and change everything?)

And then of course there's the fact that Microsoft could enter the DaaS market themselves, offering Windows desktops and applications as a service from Azure via Project Mohoro (or whatever they'll call it). What would happen if Microsoft did that? Could anyone compete with them? Would your DaaS provider survive?

Sure, this isn't exactly their bread and butter, but CEO Satya Nadella is a cloud guy, Azure has been gaining traction, and who better to deliver desktops as a service than the company who literally wrote the desktop software? Microsoft has the OS, the protocol, and the cloud platform. If they get the will, look out!

Combine that with Office 365 and Exchange in Azure as hosted services—not to mention other Microsoft platforms like SharePoint and Lync that can run on Windows Servers hosted in Azure and future versions of Windows Server products that will hook into Azure right out of the box—and why *wouldn't* you just put your server-hosted desktops there? And even though a lot of people really hate Microsoft, we're stuck in their desktop environment for now, so why not just buy directly from the source?

Of course all this talk about Microsoft entering the DaaS market directly is just speculation. Maybe it happens. Maybe not. And even if Microsoft does enter the market, they don't exactly have the most stellar reputation when it comes to their "v1" products. Plus Microsoft has a strong partner ecosystem that they're not going to want to piss off too badly. Just like Dell and HP are fine even though Microsoft released the Surface tablet, your DaaS provider will probably be fine even if Microsoft enters the DaaS or Windows Application as a Service (WAaaS?) space (especially if you have a more bespoke environment). So maybe in that case competition from Microsoft will force your existing provider to up their game, so you win either way!

The Bottom Line: You Have to Do Something

If that's the future, what do you do in the meantime?

Even if Windows is going away, it's going away slowly, which means you have a long time to deal with this transition. You'll have Windows applications forever. The best case is that you'll be able to install them on some server and deliver them remotely, and it won't matter whether that server is on your premises or in the cloud. (Actually the best case is that you wouldn't even know!)

In the meantime, we know there are better ways to manage Windows desktops and deliver Windows applications. Some of those ways involve hosting Windows in a data center, and sometimes it makes sense to outsource the data center to someone else.

At the end of the day we don't think anyone's going to get fired by not going to DaaS right now. We believe there are lots of great reasons to use VDI, and that there are lots of great reasons to use DaaS. For now though it's still all about managing Windows desktops and applications. That's going to be your focus for the foreseeable future, regardless of whether you deliver Windows the traditional way, via VDI, or via DaaS. Just don't hold off on doing something because Windows might go away soon. That's not happening.

So that's our book. Thanks for giving us your money.

Appendix. 204 Questions to Answer Before Migrating to DaaS

It seems like in many ways, this book poses more questions than it answers. Realizing that, we pulled out every question from this entire book and assembled them into this huge list here. Some of the questions are things that you have to answer yourself, and others are questions that you need to ask your potential DaaS providers.

You'll find as you read through them that they may not all apply to your environment, and you might not be able to answer them all right now, but they should provide a good starting point as you consider and plan your move to DaaS.

Questions to Ask Yourself

- Why are you moving to DaaS?
- DaaS is remote Windows desktops, just like VDI or RDSH from the cloud. Are you ready for this?
- Do your users need to connect to full remote desktops, or is connecting to single remote applications more appopriate?
- Have you tried RDSH or VDI internally?
- If so, do you have lessons learned you can apply to your DaaS environment?
- If not, are you sure you know what you're getting into?
- If you tried and failed at VDI, why do you think you'll be successful with DaaS?
- If you're doing VDI currently, why do you need DaaS?
- DaaS is a desktop migration. Are you ready for this?
- Which version of Windows will you migrate to?
- Which users will you migrate?
- Have you found a provider you trust?
- Where are your users' files going to live? In your data center? On a server at your DaaS provider's location? In a cloud service like Dropbox?
- Are you prepared to make changes to your network?
- Can your existing network handle the additional traffic load of DaaS?
- Can your existing WiFi environment handle every user bringing in two or three devices?
- How will you audit and assess your existing desktops for usage patterns and applications?
- What are you doing for user profiles?

- How are you handling user authentication?
- How are you handling printing?
- Are you prepared for the potential licensing changes?
- Do you have an exit strategy?
- Even if you're ready for DaaS, should you do it?

Questions to Ask Your DaaS Provider

Security

- How do they handle user security?
- How do they handle password resets? (Both for your users and for your admins.)
- How do they secure your network, data, and disk images?
- Do they have a plan in case the equipment is seized for legal reasons?
- Do you put a domain controller onsite?
- Do you hook into your own domain, or do they have a domain that your users authenticate to?
- If you use their domain, is that somehow connected to your domain? Identity management? Federation?
- If you use their domain for some reason, who creates users and manages groups?
- What about two-factor authentication?
- How does the DaaS provider authenticate you as a person? How do they know you are who you say you are when you call to make image changes? What about when your users call with a problem?

- What if you have proof that someone is spying on your desktops or stealing your data?
- Do you have the legal ability to go after the thieves in that locality?
- Will the local government support you?
- Who owns the physical facility where your provider's DaaS infrastructure lives?
- How is their facility secured?
- Who has physical access to the infrastructure?
- Do they have admin rights to your desktops?
- Are you able to audit who from the DaaS provider accessed your environment and to see what they did?
- How are your desktops isolated from other customers' desktops? Are you each on separate hardware? Or just separate VMs on the same hardware? Or just separate sessions on the same VM?
- When users log in, how do you know they're booting up or connecting to one of your desktops? How does the provider protect against "desktop in the middle" attacks?
- How do you know that your disk image hasn't been compromised?
- How do you know that someone hasn't tampered with it or installed screen recording or key recording software into your image?
- Do they offer drive or disk image encryption? If so, who has the keys?
- Are you on the same network as other customers?
- How is the isolation of networks done?
- Does the DaaS provider's management network cross over into your DaaS environment, or is it separate?

Infrastructure & Platform

- Do they have IaaS/PaaS services as well? Will they?
- Can they integrate with other IaaS/PaaS providers you might already work with?
- What DaaS platform are they using?
- Is the DaaS provider consumer- or enterprise-focused?
- What OS will you be using?
- Can the OS be tweaked to look like a client version of Windows?
- What happens if the DaaS desktops don't perform as well as you wanted? Who troubleshoots that?
- Will they proactively notify you of poor performance, or do they wait until a user calls to complain?
- What is backed up?
- Can you add more to the list of what's backed up?
- Can you back up less?
- Can you turn backup off altogether?
- How often does backup occur? Can you change that?
- Can you restore just certain files?
- Can you even do restores? Or do you have to contact the DaaS provider?
- Can the users do self-restores?
- If you leave the DaaS provider, will they delete your backups? Can they prove it?
- Do they work with other providers for backup/high-availability purposes? (If so, every question on this entire list should apply to them as well.)
- Should you back up your images and data to your office?

- Can they help you estimate the size of your internet bandwidth requirements?
- Do you share storage with your competitors?
- Do they have an application publishing solution rather than just desktops?

Clients & Users

- Does the provider have recommendations for thin clients?
- What remote desktop protocol are they using?
- Do they have their own software clients?
- What endpoint devices do they support? (PC, Mac, Android, iOS?)
- What use cases make the most sense in your DaaS provider's environment?
- What are some use cases where customers have had issues?
- Can your users install their own applications?

Image & Application Management

- Why does Microsoft licensing suck? (Seriously, does the DaaS provider have any ideas? Because we don't.)
- Do they provide Office licenses as part of their package?
- Have they run into non-Microsoft applications whose licenses are not compatible with DaaS?
- What is the image creation process?
- Do they offer templates you can use? Or guides to creating template images?
- Is there a limit to image size?

- What "optimizations" are being made to the images by the provider?
- How flexible are they to make any changes to their cookie-cutter solutions?
- How much desktop management does the provider do? What is left to you?
- Do they support persistent, non-persistent, or both types of images?
- How many master image templates for different types of users can you have?
- Do they use layering? Do you create the layers, or do they? Who assigns the layers?
- If you're using non-persistent desktops, how do you handle user-installed applications? What about regression testing?
- Do they use application virtualization? Do you have access to it?
- Do they use user environment management? Do you have access to it?
- Will they notify you first before they touch your desktops?
- Do they only do things that you ask them to? Or do they have the ability (or can you give them permission) to react to certain things?
- Can they make changes to the image without notifying you?
- Who patches the desktops?
- Who patches applications?
- Can you ask the DaaS provider not to patch your images?
- Can they overrule you and deploy a critical patch?
- If the DaaS provider is providing support for applications, will they also let you install your own applications?

- What happens if one of the applications you install breaks one of their applications?
- What if one of the DaaS provider's updates breaks one of your user-installed applications?
- Whose antivirus do you use?
- Can you use your own antivirus?
- Can you tweak antivirus settings?
- If they use the same antivirus as you, can you hook their antivirus into your system?
- Who is responsible for troubleshooting outages?

Network & Data

- Do they cache network data or files? How long is that cache in place for? Can you turn that off? Can you ensure it's cleared when or if you leave this provider?
- How do you get your data back from the DaaS provider if you decide to stop doing DaaS?
- If you leave the DaaS provider, will they delete your backups? Can they prove it?
- Where in the world will your desktops be hosted?
- Where in the world will your data be hosted?
- Do they have their own cloud storage solution? Does it integrate with your file servers too?
- What data should you move or replicate? My Documents? Shared drives? All of it?
- Does the DaaS provider have access to your data?
- Does the DaaS provider have access to your network?
- If you use roaming profiles, do they suggest you pull those across the internet or host them locally?
- How does printing work?

- Can you host a print server at the provider? Should you?

Costs

- Is there a charge for data transfers for inter-data-center communications? File replication? App traffic?
- Are there any additional charges for internet usage?
- Is there a cost for hosting storage at the DaaS provider?
- Is there a cost for hosting a domain controller or other service at the provider?
- Should you replicate all your local data or carve off just what you need to support those users you have in DaaS?
- Are the costs different for persistent versus non-persistent desktops?
- Are the costs different for RDSH sessions versus VMs per user?
- Does the provider's cost include Windows licenses? Which ones?
- Do they charge differently for maximum concurrent users versus total named users?
- If you pay for a certain number of users, do they have enough capacity for all these users to be active at the same time?
- Does the provider's cost include Office licenses?
- Do you have to pay sales tax?
- Do you get a discount for paying all at once?
- Do you get a discount for a longer term contract?
- What are the penalties for breaking a contract?
- What's the refund policy?

Trust

- If files/desktops are hosted in multiple countries, how do the laws of each country affect your environment?

- Whose laws apply if the DaaS provider is in a different city/state/country than you if there is a legal dispute?

- Are there any legal differences between your state and the state or country where the DaaS provider resides that could cause issues between you and them?

- Does your DaaS provider say they're 100% customizable? What exactly does that mean to them?

- What do they do to make sure your desktops stay running? Storage? Networking? Power? Internet? Redundancy?

- Do they have enough infrastructure and personnel to accommodate a huge customer, maybe one reacting to an emergency?

- What is their infrastructure plan? Do they wait for complaints before adding capacity, or do they stay ahead of the curve?

- What kind of security certifications do they have?

- How do you verify the integrity of their employees?

- If you administer your own servers, can the DaaS provider get back admin rights if they wanted?

- Which exact parts of your environment are under the control of the DaaS provider?

- Will you get dedicated support before, during, and/ or after migration?

- Can they help you create an exit strategy?

- What does their SLA guarantee?

- Can you customize your SLA?
- What happens if the provider doesn't meet the SLA?
- Can they tell you a story about the last outage they had? How long was it? How were customers impacted? What have they done to ensure it won't happen again?
- How long is their typical outage?
- Are you compensated for outages? How?

Made in the USA
Middletown, DE
28 October 2014